PROMO MONKEY

MY LIFE AS A BELLHOP IN THE WALDORF HYSTERIA

Friends & Enemas

RayMan Ramsay

FriesenPress

One Printers Way
Altona, MB R0G 0B0
Canada

www.friesenpress.com

Copyright © 2022 by RayMan Ramsay
First Edition — 2022

My original intention was to run away and be a Pirate (hmm, close!) but decided to run off and join the Rock & Roll circus instead, and I survived!

All rights reserved.

No part of this publication may be reproduced in any form, or by any means, electronic or mechanical, including photocopying, recording, or any information browsing, storage, or retrieval system, without permission in writing from FriesenPress.

ISBN
978-1-5255-9971-2 (Hardcover)
978-1-5255-9970-5 (Paperback)
978-1-5255-9972-9 (eBook)

1. MUSIC, GENRES & STYLES

Distributed to the trade by The Ingram Book Company

To my friend, Ches...
White Rocks son!

[signature]

PROMO MONKEY

Let it be known that, partial proceeds of the sale of this Epic

Go to Wigs for Kids (BC)
In support of BC Children's Hospital
….to put a smile on a child.

www.wigsforkidsbc.com

Tah for your kind coinsideration

RayMan

What *is* the *Promo Monkey* series?

A selection of real life/hands on working experiences from my time as a Promo Rep/Manager over 36 years between Quality Records/TPC distribution and the RCA/BMG experience in the Vancouver and BC markets as well as anecdotal stories of some of the most famous music artists and performers in the world and possibly in the galaxy, if you count people like David Bowie.

Honorable Menschens to the Creative Spirit that let me in, and to all my Music Buds that took the journey back then and by guile, gall, hand, heart, and mind, sound or otherwise, that had the Will, Persistence, Tenacity, and Desire to succeed back when it was still fun, yeah.

PROMO MONKEY:
MY LIFE AS A BELLHOP IN THE WALDORF HYSTERIA CHATTERS

#1- A&R, ABBA, Bryan Adams, Ad Infinitum, Christina Aguilera, Bruce Allen, Paul Alofs, Asian Culture Media, Julian Austin, Ken Bain, Carroll Baker, Long John Baldry

#2- Bhangra, Backstreet Boys, BigFoot, Bobby Taylor & the Vancouvers, Bruce Bissell, Spencer Britten, BMG Van, Brooks & Dunn (& Reba)

#3- Randy Bachman, BTO (Bachman Turner Overdrive), Brave Belt, Blu Cantrell, Canadian Idol/Ryan Malcolm, Blu Cantrell, CCR, Charity/Chemo Savvy, Dave Chesney, Curt Cobain, Commander Cody, Warren Copnick, Copyright, Cowboy Junkies, Crash Test Dummies

#4- Classic Convention/Paul White, Bobby Curtola/Bo Diddly, Dave Matthews Band, Conan Daly, John Denver, Dido, Doug & the Slugs, Doomsbury, Elvis, Entertainment Consultant

#5- Eurythmics, Everlast, Fabs/Beatles, Sam Feldman, Fergie (pre-Peas), Fintry Queen, Fleetwood Mac/Bucking Nicks, John Ford, Radney Foster.

#6- Grammys 1985, Jefferson Starship,

#7- David Gray, Buddy Guy, Hall & Oates, Emmy-Lou Harris, Hats, The Higgins/Patty Griffin, Bruce Hornsby, Whitney Houston/Cissy Houston, Hudson Brothers, Terry Jacks, Alan Jackson, Jake.

#8- Colin James, Bob Jamieson. Jeff Healy Band, Jingle Cats, Billy Joel, (Sir)Elton John, Carolyn Dawn Johnson, Tom Jones, The Judds, Juno Awards/Rascalz

#9- Lemmy Kilmister, Gene Kiniski, KISS, Avril Lavigne, Led Zeppelin/ Rachael Yamagata, Carlton Lee, Lying, The Lincolns, Dee Lippingwell,

#10- Loverboy, LoverGirl (Lynne), Lynyrd Skynyrd, The Macarena, Larry MacRae (Lawrence-of-a-Radio), Ray McAuley & Wild Country

#11- Martina McBride, Terry McBride, Craig McDowell, Kris McKay/ My Sugarman, Catherine McKinnon, McMaster & James, Murray McLauchlan, Charlie Major, Bob Marley, Maroon 5, Matthew Good

#12- Metaforest

#13- MRB/Midnite Rodeo Band, Bonnie James, Anne-Marie de la Giroday, Moby, Ed Molyski, Monty Python

#14- Me, and Cancer

#15- Van Morrison, Mötley Crüe/Autograph, Mr Mister, Terry Mulligan

#16- Dave Matthews Band, Ted Wendland/Hansie

#17- Mike Ness, Newton Inn, NSYNC/Boy oh Boy Bands, New York Dolls, Odds (My FAVORITE Band), Original Swing Kids, Beth Orton

#18- Owls

#19- Parachute Club, Parking, Dolly Parton, Passion, Hugh Pickett

#20- Nestor Pistor

#21- Powder Blues, Prairie Oyster, Pointer Sisters, Presenting.../BCCMA inducted to Hall of Fame

#22- The Press, Ed Preston, Suzi Quatro, Radio, Ray's Idea Orphanage, RCA, Rascalz, Reggae, Bill Reiter, Red Robinson, Respect.

#23- Raynaissance- what started this party, Kenny Rogers, Romeo's Daughter (for crying out loud!), Diana Ross.

#24- Elvis, "That's Alright" (and it's NOT!), Rock-a-Billy/Robert Gordon, Royalty: Music & Otherwise, Kings of Leon, Santana, SaveOnFoods: More?, Andrea True & the Truth be told/Phornographic Records, Bev Shannon, Billy Joe Shaver, Shelly Siegel.

#25- Poco/Eagles, TV Tunes.

#26- Chris Rea, Shipwreck/Monuments Galore, jacksoul, Bloody Chiclets, Big House, There's a fine line…, Six Cylinder, Skin, Sloan, Jo-El Sonnier, Red Sovine

#27- Britney Spears, Spontaneity: Paul/Heckler, Keith/Chuck, Howling Wolf/Eric Clapton, Rick Springfield, Stage Mothers, Stampeders, Kentish Steele, Steps, Cat Stevens, Michelle Stewart

#28-Sir Monty Rock III, Skiffle/Lonnie Donegan, Stonebolt, Stone Roses, (Rolling) Stones, Donna Summer, Sunset Bombers/Jay Lasker

#29-Thompson Twins, Thor, Justin Timberlake, Tool/ Urban Dance Squad, Toronto, The TPC Crew, The Tractors, Traffic/Jim Capaldi, Tragically Hip

#30-Treachers Records, Treble Charger, Trooper

#31-T.Rex, Tuesday (Label)/Steel River, Bruce Allen/Crosstown Bus, Shelly Siegel

#32-Tune toons, Dame Evelyn Glennie

#33-Under the Influences: Harry Belafonte, Little Richard, Leon Russell, & MORE, Vangelis

#34-Vanilla Ice, Snap, Puff Daddy/P. Diddy, Notorious B.I.G. (Christopher Wallace)

#35-Waylon (Jennings) & Willie (Nelson), Kitty Wells, White Rabbit (The Song), The Who/Powder Blues, Wilbur Harrison/Lee Michaels, Roger Whittaker

#36-Hank Williams Sr/Jr, Shed Wooley (Ben Colder), Michelle Wright, Yes, Yanni, Warren Zevon /Odds, Lisa Z.

PROMO MONKEY

MY LIFE AS A BELLHOP IN THE WALDORF HYSTERIA

Friends & Enemas

By RayMan Ramsay

Copyright by ALadinLadner:
the Written Werd & Dirty Book Store Publishing

FORE!.....

Promo Monkey...explained

This was an accident, not at all planned.

I had retired (Raytired) from working for record labels, the last being **BMG** (Bertelsmann Music Group), which I started with when it was **RCA Canada** (1977), which then became **RCA Ariola** (I know, it sounds like yodeling, but the owners were German, not Swiss), then **RCA/BMG**, then just **BMG**, and finally, "Extinct," having been swallowed headlong by one **Sony Music**; in Business, this is called a "Merger," rhymes with murder.

Having said that, since this was written, **BMG** has resurrected itself as a label entity of considerable power.

As I had begun this epic journey on April 1, 1968, with **TPC** (Taylor, Pearson, Carson), the **Quality Records** distributor, I realized, as 2013 approached, that date would mark my 45 Anniversary in the Music Bidness. To celebrate that, I thought I would inflict a one page/one time note of my careen hilites to my Music/Media Buds that I continued to have contact with, and carefully drew up a list of victims. You see, altho I had "retired" in June 2004, I NEVER left the Music; in fact, if my DNA Helix is examined I'm pretty sure it will be full of music notes, and a sea of red ink, yeah.

The response to this initial nuclear Missive was pretty substantial: Encore!

The poor bastards.

So **My Special Music People** (now **Promo Monkey**) was borne.

It's not chronological, it's alphabetical by Group, Artist, Project, or Personality, which has posed challenges along the way. For example, if I'm writing in the M's and I recall something in the B's, I have to be clever to find a way to make it fit.

On the other hand, while these started out as capsule items, some subjects just needed more leg room, and became a Supplement now **Promo Monkey: Monkey See, Monkey TWO**.

I still, to this day, have "Oh YEAH! I *HAVE* to include (whatever)" moments, so the book still continues to write itself, altho the version you're reading is as complete as possible to this date.

This opus went on for 36 chapters over 2 years, plus 7 years of the ensuing "Integrity" and many supplements (now all integrated) of length. That's a LOT of writing!

This NEW version, which merges all the original stories and chapters into one story entitled "**Promo Monkey: My Life as a BellHop in the Waldorf Hysteria- Friends & Enemas**"" and the follow up "**Promo Monkey: Monkey See, Monkey Two-Personas & Prima Donnas-** has been a labour of lust, and while the original versions had few links to further ignite the reader's interest, this version does, but mostly makes Recos/Recommendations rather than clickable links as it is a hard copy book after all

I have taken some flak for the way I relate or portray the history, randomly, from my side of the writer's desk (The Emperors Clothier), but I defend my write to interpretation, as I tend to err on the side of *Passion* rather than Caution, and Damn the Tomatoes!

It has been a fabulous journey and continues to be exciting. I am extremely fortunate, if not outright Blessed or blissed, to be on it.

I LOVE writing, and I LOVE Music (and the business of). It was *ALWAYS* about the Music, always.

Now...here's your peek behind the curtain, looking back thru the Looking Glass...

RayMan Ramsay

....WORD!

CHATTER #1

A BRIEF RAYCAP OF MY CAREER IN A ~~NUTHOUSE~~, NUTSHELL.

A Short List of some of the SPECIAL people and projects I worked with during my 38 Odd (and they WERE ODD!) years in the Music Bidness...

A&R-

Stands for "Artists and Repertoire," but depending on the individual, can also stand for Head Up His Ass or HuHa. I was shocked to hear one of them tell me in smug confidence that the reason **Rita McNeil** (he referred to her as "Eat a big meal," nice) wasn't signed was because she was um… unbecoming, and that'll do for what was really said. So, an opportunity to have one of Canada's biggest and best-selling recording artists and concert draws was lost to the competition. I guess that answers the question: How stupid can you get?

ABBA-

I had their FIRST record on **Playboy Records** when they were called **Bjorn &** Benny and Svenska Flicka. **NOBODY** would play it, and now? They knew it all along!

Reco- ABBA,-"People Need Love" video (1973)

BRYAN ADAMS-

A genuinely nice guy. From Sweeney Todd to being himself, hanging out in the clubs, and lusting after Tina @ The Cave. He (and Bruce) did it his way.

A brief departure if I may (and who's writing this anyway?) from the regular format with a timely inclusion of a tip of the old Helmet to Canada's **Service Veterans** of all the Wars and conflicts including **WWI and II, Korea, Vietnam** (a good many Canadians fought in that action, over 20,000, I'm informed) and the more recent War in **Afghanistan,** who tried to free a Country caught in the grip of imbeciles that call us Infidels.

In a testament to the former weekly Masthead, **My Special Music People**, two Special people indeed have permitted me to include the video link to **"Ric-A-Dam-Doo"** written by our own **Bryan Adams** and **Jim Vallance**.

These "Special People" to whom I refer bear more than a passing resemblance to my past (where I live apparently) Brethren in Arms **Bruce Allen** and (the late) **Marlene Palmer,** and while we all know Bruce, for those that haven't had the pleasure, Marlene is one of those rare and incredible Behind the scenes / Power behind the Throne people without whom good little things wouldn't get bigger.

The **"Ric-A-Dam-Doo"** feature will air on 'The National' on Nov 8 and again on Nov 11/13.

Please take a moment to peep the attached Press Release.

Enjoy the video; it will move you to tears, cheers, and acts of selflessness.

Note: There is no sound on the intro, do not adjust your set.

https://www.youtube.com/watch?v=PGIRSaIj9wY

BRYAN ADAMS & JIM VALLANCE PENNED *'RIC-A-DAM-DOO'* COMMEMORATES 100TH ANNIVERSARY OF PRINCESS PATRICIA'S CANADIAN LIGHT INFANTRY

Song Commissioned by the Right Honourable Adrienne Clarkson

Available at iTunes® from November 5th

"Hear the battle cry
See the Ric-A-Dam-Doo
It's the flag of freedom in the air
Always glorious, victorious
Standing shoulder to shoulder to the end"

(Toronto, ON – October 2013)- On November 5th, Universal Music Canada, the country's leading Music Company will release exclusively to iTunes a specially commissioned song called **"Ric-A-Dam-Doo."** Written by Bryan Adams and Jim Vallance, to commemorate the 100th anniversary in 2014 of the Princess Patricia's Canadian Light Infantry, **"Ric-A-Dam-Doo"** was composed at the request of the regiment's Colonel-in-Chief, The Right Honourable Adrienne Clarkson.

Recorded in Edmonton, Vancouver and Toronto, it is sung by the wives of the soldiers of the PPCLI, featuring two Edmonton-based singers, Brittany Hancock and Angela Larson. In addition to Remembrance Day, the song will be played as the soldiers come home later this year and next from Afghanistan. Proceeds will go to the Princess Patricia's Light Infantry Foundation, a charitable organization that provides funds, activities, and programs to support and care for Canadian military service and former military personnel in need.

"With 'Ric A Dam Doo,' Bryan Adams and the Home-Fire Choir have honoured the proud history and tradition of the Princess Patricia's Canadian Light Infantry and the 100 years that they have served Canada. I am thrilled that the release of this song and video will lead us into 2014 and the many events we have planned to commemorate the Princess Patricia's 100th Anniversary. It is an anthem that all Canadians can rally around, reminding us of the values that the Princess Patricia›s and Canadian Forces fight for. The song also underscores the responsibility that we have to take care of our soldiers when they come home from these distant lands, not just with our voices but with practical support, for they have sacrificed a great deal. Bryan himself is putting action behind the words he penned for this song by donating all proceeds to support wounded Patricia›s. ‹Ric A Dam Doo› is a song that the Princess Patricia›s and Canada will sing proudly for the next 100 years to come!» - The Right Honourable Adrienne Clarkson, Colonel-in-Chief, Princess Patricia›s Canadian Light Infantry.

The title "Ric-A-Dam-Doo" comes from the flag of the regiment. Princess Patricia of Connaught, after whom the regiment was named in 1914, was given the title of Colonel-in-Chief and designed and made by hand the crimson flag with a circular royal blue centre. Inside the circle are the gold initials VP, which stands for Victoria Patricia. It has been in place since the First World War.

Ric-a-Dam-Doo is believed to be Gaelic for "cloth of your mother".

AD INFINITUM-

In my Salad days, I was given money to buy Radio ad air time for a new album on a local Top 40 Radio Station. I was to book the time and dates the ad/spots were to run, send the hit single to the production people, give them the title of the LP and the price point for a local retailer and told the station to do the rest. I guess it turned out ok (lower case), but I didn't know any better at that point.

Being Passionate about what I was doing I decided that I COULD do better and would write the radio spots from that point on.

At the next opportunity, I took it all in hand and wrote the script, indicating emphasis for the announcer, timed out the parts of the music bed and indicated where they should go, provided a retail price point and demanded approval prior to it going to air and a copy for my office. This was a bit unheard of at the time, and I probably came on like something of an upstart know-it-all, but WHO would know better about HOW their product should be presented than the advertiser?! I was actually making it a piece of cake for the production department, and those spots sounded HOT, they did.

Encouraged by my initial success, I kept at it, moving into print layouts and even a TV spot or two. One station liked my stuff so much, their production department would call me from time to time for ideas on some other advertiser bookings; I recall the **Old Spaghetti Factory** in Gastown being one of them.

I still have a collection of radio spots on cassette and like a Leopard, I wouldn't change them. All in all (Cue Paul Anka), I did it **My Way.**

CHRISTINA AGUILERA-

The Ice Queen. Brilliant vocalist. Caused a Vancouver Media Shitstorm by leaving an autograph session and a Radio Station's contest winners out in the cold to go shopping and had people in **NY** yelling for my head. Nice. Also the first time I had to look in my promo budget for candy...sigh. Kids with money.

She made an encore of her behavior performance in Edmonton, turning the efforts by my Promo Bud Conan and the Alberta crew a freaking nightmare; what a bitch.

BRUCE ALLEN-

I grew up in the biz with him and Sam, who was the Mel Tormé phone voice to Bruce's Joe Cocker. Some people fear him, but he has always been a great guy to me. He respects hard work and honesty (if you haven't got THAT, you got NOTHIN'). Even when he YELLED at me, I YELLED back; we laughed and we fine.

PAUL ALOFS-

A Good man, believed in me and gave me BMG's 1st and only Inspiration Award.

ASIAN MEDIA-

Once I got a full-time assistant and made it to **Promotions/Media Relations Manager** (and sometimes Branch Manager), I had a bit of time to look for new outlets to promote and expose our Music, and took aim at Asian Media to try and tap that market some more. After all, they have money too, and like to be entertained, so why not include them so they can buy OUR stuff! This was not easily done, however; after more than a century of being marginalized & mistreated by white people, they tended to keep to themselves and were very insular, and who could blame them?

So, it took a while to earn their trust and respect and show that my efforts weren't designed to rip them off of what was theirs. I eventually got thru with a good deal of honesty & respect and even tried to learn some of the language as a show of that. I could say very small phrases, but they liked that and let me in.

I never promised them something I couldn't deliver, and in return they gave me ACRES of press, and Rivers if not an Ocean of ink, *COLOURED* INK. I could never read a word, had no clue what they were saying about the product, but it sure looked good, and it WORKED. I kept these contacts up and still use them for my Charity Media work, again to good effect; it's all about *inclusion.*

JULIAN AUSTIN-

A good ol' boy (and a good ol' boy was he!). We'd been on the road doing promo for his new album and before arriving at **Gabby's** in Langley. I had their bouncers join me and made a flying wedge around Julian to move him thru the crowd to the autograph area in the foyer after his mini-set; the place was PACKED. We had it going good, the fans came up, he made his "x" they got a pic and NEXT!...until one Snuff Queen came up in a noticeably altered state and suddenly went all Mike Tyson on him, jumped into his lap and bit his ear, hard!

Why would you do that...branding?

So, we got "Jaws" off Julian and we all figured this Harpy should be thrown into a Hay Baler, but thought the better of it and sent her back to the bar without the damn good spanking she deserved.

Reco- Julian Austin, "Little Ol' Kisses" video.

Also, the (Cowboy) re-Boot of "Take the Money and Run," yeah, THAT one.

KEN BAIN-

A **TRUE** BMG Buddy. I loved to Lord over him the fact we have "**White Spot**" and T.O. doesn't. He was a Repository for White Spot coffee cups, paper bags, napkins and (empty) burger containers, which we sent him via the company courier. To him, it was Aromatherapy.

CARROLL BAKER-

Real nice lady. When I started at **RCA**, I worked with her so much I thought I was going to look like her, which would have been weird, me with a Platinum Blonde Wig and Boobs. Her Manager, **Don Grashey**, got **Loretta Lynn** started (she lived just across the border in Lyndon, Washington back then) and probably wore the same sports jacket all his life. Carroll was into exercising with music way ahead of its time, could do deep knee bends like nobody's business. People who want to genuflect with gusto could learn something from her.

LONG JOHN BALDRY-

LOVED his *It Ain't Easy* LP and was a bit in awe of him when I met him. This was with TPC/Quality, and he did two LPs for **Casablanca**. I first met him at his gig at **The Old Roller Rink** club in North Vancouver. Didn't work with him too often, which was good for my neck, looking way up at him all the time. His Management Company was called "**Piranha**," and that was more than apt.

CHATTER#2

BHANGRA-

This music form started as a form of East Indian Folk music, which quickly turned into an early type of Trance music, Bhang being the term for Hashish. **BMG** picked up the rights to **Musicor Records** from the UK, which was the modern form of the format. I found it shocking how, without reservation, a lot of Video/Music store owners would bend over their own Culture by booting a song at the drop of headwear, and think nothing of it.

Part of the Musicor package was a local artist going by the name of **Indian Lion**, **Michael Sunner** by day, and he defined himself as more of a Pop artist, and distanced himself from the "Bhangra cache." It was a challenge to work this, given his past relations with the South Asian Media, which were a bit strained and estranged, you might say, and his Manager was a lot of work too…**La De Da**. I stopped working with him when I realized my calls were being recorded.

We DID get some feature Top 40 play, but nothing like **Apache Indian's** *Arranged Marriag*e got.

I did go to a Bhangra concert involving a couple of **Musicor** groups, and it was a real eye-opening Cultural experience to see how they worked their own community, but I couldn't help feel like the center of an Oreo cookie.

BACKSTREET BOYS-

A non-starter here at first, but some unique promo jump-started it. This act broke out of Montreal in North America; **Stephane Drolet** did that, and THEN they broke in the U.S. They were NEVER a BAND, they were a Vocal Group, The Beatles were a "Boy" BAND.

There was a Post-Concert "After Party" fiasco with **BSB** (No! I WON'T say their whole name again!) at **Cheers,** a licensed bar in North Delta, which I had heard about on the radio. I called their Management, who don't bother checking with local Label Reps at all and they confirmed it. I asked if they knew where it was and they told me it was *right* beside the venue. Noooooo, it isn't, it isn't even in the same city, it's about 40 minutes away at least...**WHAT!?** they said, and I'm pretty sure I could hear assholes banging shut at this news, but they assured me they could handle it. Fine.

Then, a little later, I heard the afternoon jock on mighty Radio Z95 throwing to this as an ALL AGES EVENT!...are you *CRAZY*!!!!!! I got hold of the jock and told him to **STOP saying that,** kids were at risk here. I also called the PD (Program Director) at home, and he followed up on it for me with the on-air guy, but the damage was done.

So now the kids get networking as well as pleading with their parents (or not) to take them to the parking lot of a bar where people are full of booze and let them hang around for as long as it takes to get a glimpse of the BSB. Finally came a tour bus inching its way thru a packed parking lot; it stops, and a whole two BSBs get out and go into the bar to be seen for about 20 minutes, then Bye Bye, back on the bus and gone like smoke. The club PAID them American $ for this, sound more like the Cash Street Boy$.

The best thing was that nobody got hurt, whew!

More BSBS: At another concert in Van, there was a Special Private Meet & Greet with the Boys put on by a breakfast cereal company; winners got to go to a hotel downtown and meet the guys one on one, a nice prize! It would seem that whoever organized this (**NOT Z95,** they were given the contest as a package) couldn't see the forest for the trees because of having stars in their eyes, as no sooner had the contest ended than they went ahead and announced to the world the name of the hotel instead of keeping it under wraps; what were they thinking??!! They shud have arranged to pick these kids up and bussed them to the hotel on the down low, but now the word is out and so are all the kids on busy Burrard Street to the point traffic wasn't moving.

While the breaky num-nums people were covering themselves in Glory, it was extremely fortunate that it didn't turn Gory as no kids were reported harmed, which was also fortunate for all the partners (BSB, BMG, Z95, the Breakfast flakes, & the Hotel), as the blowback would have been tragic otherwise, and everyone would be having Crow for breakfast instead of cereal.

AGAIN **with the BSB**: One of the activities for a Vancouver concert involved them singing the American National Anthem at an AFL/CFL football game at BC Place Stadium, another something signed and sealed over our (local) heads: once again, no consultation.

To this day, I have no idea who disorganized, this event but the "Presents" for this Pigskin extravaganza was given to the Radio Station **The Fox**, who we know is Vancouver's **RAWK** Station.

I got a call that afternoon from their Tour Manager asking me if I could escort them to the BC Place stadium; I told him to step out the back door of (then) GM Place and look across the street, waaaaay over there, and he would see the back doors to BC Place, he could hit it with a rock… aaaaaah, thanks!

Don't thank me, this is gonna get worse.

So they hopped in their Limo and motored all the way across the street, go in the rear entrance and onto the field to be **BOOED** right off the AstroTurf by all **The Fox** listeners in attendance who simply HATED them…Oh say can you see a way outta here! Oh, this was televised too, uh huh. So, they did their bit then wisely fled with a big bag o' cash. Aside from bruised egos, nobody got hurt.

Promo Monkey: My Life as a BellHop in the Waldorf Hysteria

Two great Radio guys and Me–(L) Z95 PD Eric Samuels and (R) MD Curtis Strange, Me in center w Z95 sticker, presenting them with Backstreet Boys' multiple platinum in 1990.

Without them, just BS.

BIGFOOT-

My band; learned how to play well with others, write songs, gained empathy for working with future Artists and groups. Bruce & Sam booked us and opened a door for the future too.

I was the drummer; I knew right off that I couldn't get an electric shock playing the wooden drums! I played guitar just enough to be able to write songs, but not on stage.

I also sang the Stones' songs cuz Jagger can't sing either, projects well though.

We had some pretty talented players thru our various configurations; one was **John Pearson,** who played Sax with us in our **Rhythm & Blues All-Stars** days; we weren't, but we wanted to be. John took the name, we vacated, and with **Colin Weinmaster** formed "**The R&B All-Stars**," huh, with **Hans Staymer** on Vocals.

The other constant thru everything was my friend **Jerome Walliser (Down Home Jerome)** who played guitar/vocals and wrote "**Out in the Street**," the band's best non-cover song; the recording is from a rehearsal. John and Colin went on to form **Wave Productions** and have been very successful.

Reco- BigFoot, "Out in the Street": https://youtu.be/B0RH-qMp12c

Jerome is in the Movie Biz and I saw him in "**The 5 People You Meet in Heaven**," an emotional book and film tour de force, quite unusual for both to be as good as the other.

I freely admit that I am probably the world's WORST guitar player, not a virtuoso, more of an OH So so-so, and certainly the slowest. I would play only the slow songs because I had to pause while I changed chords, and I wouldn't do that often...*CHANGE* chords?! *YOU* change chords! I *LIKE* this chord and I'm gonna STAY here! Like I said, drummer.

I would have been VERY popular at a Dirge-Fest: "Hey, where's Ray, I need to cheer down!"

A friend of mine recently commented on my LinkedIn picture, saying I looked like **Eric Clapton.** I replied that I played guitar like **Eric Claptrap.**

Back in those days, there weren't any monitors, and sitting behind the rest of the band thumping the tubs, with all the music going AWAY from me,

I'd say we were lucky if we were playing the same songs. It was a joyful noise, if not an outright racket, **Beethoven's 9th Racket** p'raps.

BOBBY TAYLOR & THE VANCOUVERS-

From Hometown to Motown...

Vancouver has never been short on talent, be it Pop, Rock or Country, and it's always been an R&B town, always. The talent needed time to grow, and so did the support industry around it.

Thru various configurations, **Bobby Taylor & the Vancouvers** emerged. Some of the members included **Bobby, Duris Maxwell** (for whom God invented drums and who would go on to keep very good time with the seminal Powder Blues), **Robbie King** (the King of the Keys!), **Wes Henderson,** and **Tommy Chong**, among others. Tommy would go on to partner with a Man named **Cheech** and the rest, as they say is hilarity!

Tommy also co-wrote their BIG hit **"Does Your Mama Know About Me?"** The group being a mix of Black, White and Chinese (Tommy) and the song, back in the day before the proliferation of Video and present-day technology, had a bit of a subliminal social message, especially to those that had yet to see them, as they were an interracial group singing to mostly white people and girls in particular, so two civil rights make a Right ON!

They were also the first mixed race group to be signed to **Motown,** and they were all OURS!

BRUCE BISSELL-

Mr. Silly to me, but NO Clown at Promotion! A **GREAT** guy, friend and survivor of da biz. Worked for **A&M** and **Weiner Bros** and he's got stories!

SPENCER BRITTEN (POST-RAYTIREMENT PROJECT)-

I'm certainly jaded after all these years, but this kid blew me away at a "Celebration of Life"; I was attending the event for my late Sister-in-law when a young Chinese kid stands up and starts singing IN ITALIAN what turned out to be **"Bring him home"** from **"Les Miserables."** I had some experience with this format from working with **Gino Vannelli's "Songs for My Father"** project, and this, to me, is every bit as good. Needs a bit of polishing, but otherwise he's a light in the forest. Also turns out we're related thru marriage. Where is **David Foster** when you need him?! Amazing.

Reco- Spencer Britten, "Bring him home": https://www.youtube.com/watch?v=VO9tHNX6L04

THE BMG VANCOUVER CREW-

Buck, Miss Katherine, Lisa, Matt2, Mike, Deano, Sean, Peter Mouser, Marilyn, Lynne, Mel, Charlotte, Michelle and Bob: ALL among the BEST crew I have worked with. RIP Leagh Alden.

BROOKS & DUNN (AND REBA) ~

Dunn now, but not forgotten. More true Country Music Pros. Country acts are SO good to work with, and they put up with a LOT.

One tour was sponsored by a brewery with a stop in Vancouver. We had to go to the brewery's hospitality suite to meet the boys.

The B&D crew were VERY well organized, as usual; the rollout was… Shake/Howdy, Pose/Click, Grin/Agin!

Each person was to receive a colour Polaroid inserted in a pre-signed cardboard frame, very nice.

Except, one of the Beer Girls had waaay too much brew (and not enough exposure to celebrities, TV and magazines notwithstanding) and spilled even more ALL OVER the table the cameras and cardboard frames were on; "Ooopsy, giggle," offered Miss Jiggle.

There was a moment of **DEAD** silence in the room, time stopped and you could hear a firing-pin drop, BUT not a discouraging word (altho *I* heard it, mind reader that I am), Kix and Ronnie just bit down HARD and got thru it.

They came thru another time on a Co-Headline show with **Reba McEntire**, and all three did the Meet & Greet together, no Burpo, slips or miss-haps(sic), and Reba was VERY nice to deal with. She was repped by Universal's **Theresa Blackwell**, who is a Super person and deserved MUCH better than she actually got in the end.

Unfortunately, **Brooks & Dunn** went on first and after their HIGH energy show, you could feel the energy level plummet as Reba came on. She does a good show, just not as dynamic as **B&D** outgunning Tres Hombres (**ZZ Top**).

(L>R:Reba, fan, Lisa/BMG's Mom, Ronnie, Lisa, Power Behind the Throne yours truly behind Lisa, Kix in a shirt that would stop traffic, and my long-suffering wife and BMG'r Lynne) Photo- Tour Management

Reco- Brooks & Dunn, "Mama Don't Get Dressed Up for Nothin'"

CHATTER #3

BTO-

Randy always a gentleman. Met up w them at the end of **Brave Belt** when **Quality** wanted a deal w them (having had Randy in **Guess Who**), but **Bruce Allen** had bigger & better ideas. Never forget them jamming w **The Stampeders** @ **Pharaohs Retreat**.

They were all **BIG** guys. The drummer, Robbie was the smallest; it looked like the others had been eating his food. They thinned out somewhat when **Blair Thornton** joined them.

"CANADIAN IDOL"-

I couldn't care less for ANY of the "Idol" TV shows, my favorite "Idol" is **BILLY Idol**. It was good TV, not so good record sales.

My first exposure to a **Canadian Idol** was the first one, **Ryan Malcolm**, who was unschooled and FULL of himself, so much so that if he fell OFF himself, he risked serious injury. Before "Idol," he was known as "Waiter?"; now it's "Hey! Waiter!"

The guy that followed Ryan, **Kalan Porter**, looked like a singing sheep, but I didn't know him. I posted Ryan's LP jacket in our front window while we went on vacation; nobody broke in.

LOCK'EM OUT STYLE-

Blu Cantrell had a hot hit on **Arista/BMG** that defined the retribution of a woman scorned called "**Hit 'em Up Style.**" She also had a tour date in what she thought was Vancouver.

I met her diminutive Blu-ness at YVR with a limo, and took her to Radio **Z95** for an on-air interview to bump her date.

We arrived as their office was closing, and went straight on-air. Interview done, we all piled back into the limo, at which point the on-air Jock BURST thru the front door and banged desperately on the limo windows, saying he forgot to get an interview for their Toronto station (where she had just been), and, altho tired and annoyed, she agrees and we all troop back to the station to find the door is **LOCKED!.**

So now the on-air jock is beating a tattoo on the door and pleading, and everyone is looking at ME like this is MY fault, and I couldn't resist asking the Jock "you DO work here, right?" **FINALLY,** with just seconds to go before the record playing runs out, the last remaining staffer in the building opens the door, and we all pile in like Lemmings.

Blu gracefully does the interview, and I double check to see that nothing else has been missed, and then we leave, for real.

As we proceed to the venue with Vancouver's city lights diminishing behind us, passing fields, farms and forests, I notice Blu and entourage acting uneasy, like they're being abducted. Finally, the Tour Manager asks why we're going AWAY from Vancouver, and I break it to him that the venue is NOT even in Vancouver, it's in ANOTHER city altogether (*another* BSB moment), and he protests that he was told Vancouver, and I tell him most of our acts get that same impression (or they wouldn't have taken the date), but they are actually playing **Cheers** in **North Delta.** So, they resign themselves to being shut out of Gastown and playing AssBucket instead. There is a whole different "Hit 'em Style" going on when they finally get to the club to find the venue doesn't have the requested equipment for their show, and as their hotel actually IS in Vancouver, they opt to stay and nap in the dressing room rather than make multiple Star Treks back and forth. They never come back to play "Vancouver," this experience being less "Cheers-y" than they expected.

CCR-

I met Stu and Doug Backstage at one of their early Vancouver shows, but John & Tom were tuning up, so I missed meeting them, altho they did sign the poster. I am a HUGE fan and **Fogerty** follower; I even have their LP when they were the **Golliwogs!**

At 20, did a caricature poster of them and they signed it! It hangs in the Ramseum in our house.

CHARITY-

My longest tenure has been with **Wigs for Kids**, since 2006 when Bev called me for some advice and I jumped right in.

I've successfully used my knowledge and contacts from my time in the Biz to do good for people that need help, namely **Wig for Kids (BC)**, benefiting **BC Children's Hospital** (BCCH). Their **"Balding for dollars"** crew hired me after hearing what I'd done for **W4K** thanks to my good friend and **W4K Chair Bev Friesen.** Altho I did some very good work for BCCH, they've since taken the PR/Media Relations back inside the Corporate structure, which is probably easier to control as I can be an acquired taste, often more Go-Rilla than Guerilla in my approach.

I've also done some work for **Delta Hospital** here in Ladner with their **"Light the Way"** Campaign handling **PR/MR** and arranging the Musical Entertainment, with great success quadrupling their attendance as well as raising their Profile and a LOT of $$!

I am fortunate that I still have some good friends in the Music/Entertainment Industries that allow me access and come to the party with donations (**Annual Silent Auction** ssssh) when they're able. Their contributions help us raise money and awareness to ease the burden of families that have kids with Cancer. At one time, my daughter was in need of BCCH services so this is a way to pay back.

Early on I wrote a Poem **"Chemo Savvy"** for Bev to use, which probably still has Longfellow rolling over in his grave.

At that time, one could get "In Kind" tax receipts for your work, which helped keep the CRA from standing on my Fiscal dick, but apparently Harper's/CRA's new philosophy of **'No good deed goes unpunished'** disallows that now, BUT...we soldier on!

A few years ago, I developed a Ladner-centric Campaign that drew attention to our bucolic little burg by spotlighting local *independent* merchants and also giving them a strong chance of return business on their donations, so win-win. The results of those 4 months of effort at the **2012**

Silent Auction (no mime MC again, darn!) were a bid of $800 for the "**Experience Ladner**" Package, plus about $3000 in cash given to me by the local public, including a $500 prize I won from **Overwaitea** for conceiving the project, pushing the grand total to over $100,000+! So, it was good work, my 'Ray' job!

With the wealth of incoming big-name acts to Vancouver in the fall, I went in pursuit of one of them signing a guitar for the next Silent Auction, including **Sir Paul** for whom I rented a Seal costume (had to return it early as it was hot and itchy) to approach him, but as he was newly shed of his Uni-Ped, he may have lost interest. But, with the help of **Charlotte Mauricio** from **Warner Music** (who used to work with me at **BMG**), we got a guitar signed by the **Red Hot Chili Peppers**! Yay Charlotte!

Prior to that, I had dragged that same guitar all over **Victoria** hoping to get **John Fogerty** (in concert there) to sign it, but no luck...Hey John? That "**Old man down the road**"? That was *ME* dragging this sea anchor around for a good cause!

It's nice to have a tax break but for me, the reward is in the work, helping put a smile on a child.

CHEMO SAVVY (WITH APOLOGIES TO TONTO)

...By Ray Ramsay (if you like it, somebody else if you don't)

Harry's a boy, his hair is his joy,
And so is his buddy called Larry
But Harry fell ill, no help from the pill
And had Chemotherapy, scary!
He felt really poor, tho no longer sore
Soon Harry was no longer hairy no more!

Now he felt REALLY sad 'bout the teasing he'd had
From kids that were bad, his esteem suffered, poor Harry

If he just had a lid, be like other kids, wouldn't feel so...contrary
So he got him a wig and felt very BIG and grew stronger, exemplary!

And he played out all day in the usual way
With Larry and Jerry and Mary, and May
Now ready for bed and wearing his 'lid'
(Said his Dad)
I love every hair on the head of that kid!

Now kids like some hair, way, way, up there
Makes them happy and normal, you dig?
So contribute a sum and please help someone
Put a smile on under a wig!

DAVE CHESNEY-

A career buddy who started at his dad's (**Joe Chesney**, the **JC** in **CJJC**) Country Radio Station in Langley, and continued on to become Music Director (MD) at **CKLG/FM** (Pre-The Fox), become a **CBS** Rep, a Writer for **City Now,** and presently is Editor of on-line Newspaper **White Rock Sun** Canadas FIRST! (www.whiterocksun.com). Solid as a Rock, Country as a Front Porch.

CURT COBAIN-

Iconic Rock Star, gifted Songwriter, noted Marksman, Tragic ending.

COMMANDER CODY & HIS LOST PLANET AIRMEN-

Wow. What a band! A terrific experience and one of my first dabbles into Country. **George Frayne** was a real good guy. **Billy C Farlowe** was over the top terrific, and Bobby Black would Steel the show!

Reco- Commander Cody, "Diggy Liggy Lo"

WARREN COPNICK-

Left his job at the mega rack-jobber (sub distributor) **Handleman** for **Bertelsmann**. A great guy, but I figured out quickly that the number of Radio Stations on his "Call" list for Vancouver visits equaled the same number of holes on a golf course! Imagine *THAT*.

As of this writing, he's been with the two different but same companies (**BMG/Sony**) for 28 years, no small feat that!

Prior to that, he attended Broadcast College and he bin sick wid it evra since, and I know cuz he showed up with a near complete knowledge of both Canadian *and* American "Calls" (Radio Station Call Letters), PLUS he knew where each of their "sticks" (broadcast antennas) was located!

He finally slipped the surly bonds of Sales for a shot at **PROMOTION**. I should mention that the old-school Sales people were of the opinion that records sold by themselves or Magic and that Promotion Reps were a drain on the economy and were the first that should be let go if times got tough, as who could prove their worth? Pretty cynical.

He stuck with it and survived the dreaded BMG/Sony merger. He had solid support from then **Pres Lisa Zbitnew** and **VP Shane Carter**, who I always found to be a good guy and who took the helm when Lisa went out on her own; **see 'The Girls That Ran the Boys Club'**.

Warren rose to **Director, National Radio Promotion**, and until recently had a foot in **A&R**, but that's a heavy workload to survive, and there's now another young fellow wearing that mantle.

Warren is survived by all the people that don't have to work with him anymore; we can all be just friends now, so good for him and all the rest of us that have Blue Thumbs!

COPYRIGHT-

A very interesting project. Rock with its pants *on*. Too much media focus on Heroin and not enough said about the Music.

COWBOY JUNKIES-

Redefined "Cool." Margo was wonderful. The "**Misguided Angel**" media tempest was a shot heard 'round the music world and nearly ended my career, but I stuck it out and the truth came out; the **DEVIL** made them do it!

Reco- "Misguided Angel," "Sweet Jane," "'Cause Cheap Is How I Feel," "200 More Miles

CRASH TEST DUMMIES (CTD)-

From the street straight up, what a story, what a ride. The 1st album "*The Ghosts that Haunt Me*" and the single "**Superman's Song**" were successful from pure Belief. Later on, the "*A Worms Life*" CD started as a project of pure Make Belief and had me running around town visiting Radio Stations in a Chicken Head mask and a Worm puppet on one arm, delivering the new record inside containers of live Dew Worms!

After a spectacular ride, including a **BIG** American breakthrough, it was tragic to watch them crash & burn at the Vogue; it blew my mind that it happened.

Reco- CTD, "Superman's Song," "Keep a Lid on Things"

I used to adopt a Dirty Harry persona when I was with an artist in public to try and deter any harm coming to them; fans don't understand this can happen, and some artists simply don't want to meet the people that pay their rent. I was with **Brad Roberts** from **CTD** at the **PNE** (Pacific National Exhibition) one afternoon and they were skeded to play there that night. The Top 40 Station had a booth on the grounds and we went there for a little pre-show interview and while we were waiting a couple of girls approached and tugged on my sleeve asking, "Are you the Promoter?" Me: "No." Tug/Her: "... Are you his Manager?" Me: "No." Tug/Her: "... are you his Grandpa?" Me, to myself: "Heavy sigh...God I hate my life."

A number of Radio Stations couldn't get their heads around the sound and refused to budge on it; an example was the MD that threw the **Crash Test Dummies "Superman's Song"** I had just given him into the trash can with a bank off his office wall (he didn't "call" that). A few months later, the same single went to Number One on his and just about every other Radio Station in Canada, the CD topped the Sales chart, over 600,000 last time I looked; he **SHOULD** have "called" that bank, I laughed all the way to mine.

Not all the Dummies are in the band.

The list goes on; one should never say "**NEVER!**".

CHATTER #4

CLASSIC CONVENTION RETENTION

RCA conventions are where they exhaust their most important resource, their staff, with marathon meetings followed by **REALLY LOUD** bands playing in old condemned buildings, next to no sleep, and catering Chicken at every given opportunity, if you count eggs for breakfast (So the eggs DID come before the CHICKEN at Lunch, dinner, and afternoon tea), right up til it hits the endangered species list. Chickens must HATE conventions…"Oh naw, not again! How many eggs do I have to lay? My asshole feels like a gunshot wound!"

As part of one convention in particular, I recall what they called "workshops" where people try to conceive of new and better ways to build mousetraps, or in some of our cases, Claptraps. One workshop was focused on how better to market a Country record, which is where my character **Billy-Bob Bumstead** originated, and that was just too much **fun!** Take note of that word; I believe it left the Music Biz vernacular around the same time I did.

THEN.. we had a workshop with a BMGentleman, **Paul White**. Why Paul is so important is because, aside from being a real nice guy, he was the head of **Capitol Records Canada** when 4 guys from **Liverpool** were "crowning" on the world stage, and he was determined to get them going with LOTS of support from **EMI** in England. Paul was one to listen to **His Master's Voice** and knew a Hit/Hot act when he heard it. Canada has always been more open to British acts originally Than the U.S., be it **Cliff**

Richards (billed as England's Elvis, I'm surprised the Colonel didn't sue), or **Monty Pythons Flying Circus**, who survived the adoption of their original name '**Owl Stretching Time**, **CANADIANS** got it, first.

So it was a real treat to get the skinny on how this **FAB**ulous project broke thru from the man that was there. To quote **Conan Daly's** sonorous **John Lennon** comment…Cums as now s'prise t' May', I almost pissed myself when he said that.

So *anyways*, Paul wasn't with the **Beatles** or Capitol at that point; he was handling Special Projects for **BMG**. Quite astute on BMG's part, hedging their bets on Paul, as The Beatles were a Special Project for Capitol's British owner EMI under the label **Parlophone**, which handled basically Comedy records. To absolutely everyone's embarrassment and mortification, that's what they were booked as for their appearance on the **Ed Sullivan Show**: a Comedy act. Now, I know the lads enjoyed a good laugh, but this was over the top, and they're STILL laughing today, as am I.

But Paul's mission this day was focused on another Classic, Classical Music, and how we could broaden the audience/consumer for this type of music from Classical Musicians and aficionados (now *there's* a fruity snooty term for ya!).

People rationally see Classical Musicians (Classical People in general as a dour lot), upper crust, monied, toffee-nosed snots. BUT the format exists, and how do we do better with it? I came up with the concept of "**Music You Didn't Know You Knew.**" A lot of people have heard the theme song for *The Lone Ranger* TV show, which is the "**William Tell Overture**," for example, so I suggested they market a sampler that actually **RE**-introduced the listener to the music and connect the Muse with the Musicians and Composers (altho most of them were dead, so possibly Decomposers is a better fit here) via a sampler of Sturm & Drang warhorses. I do confess, I **LOVE** Strauss waltzes, back in HIS day, his shit was like "**Dark Side of the Moon**" is to us.

Classic Classics Music you didn't know you knew!

Get Bach!
Old Time Chopin Roll
Roll Over Beethoven
Go for Baroque
Back in My Brahms Again

On Top of Vivaldi
Paint My Wagner

Like a lot of my ideas, nothing came of this, it went straight to my "**Ray's Bright Idea Orphanage**" where they all die of inattention...Dearly Beloved, we are gathered here to appease Ray cuz you know how he gets...

Like any Label Rep, I've done my time touring with Classical Artists and Musicians...Carrying the Irish Flautist (he played the FLUTE, read a book!) **James Galway's** computer thru Van Int'l Airport, and in those days computers were the size of a mini-bar (my BACK!!), and carrying **Myron Floren's** accordion thru the same airport (oh no! let *ME* carry that). What the hell was I thinking! It weighed like a sea anchor! Just ask my separated shoulder.

I also recall having the Piano Virtuoso **Evgeny Kissin**, a Russian, (I called him "Huggin' and Kissin'," in English). I had some communication problems with him, as he only spoke Russian, and one required an interpreter to communicate, and you could only hope the interpreter liked you or you had NO idea what he was telling the guy, PLUS, I couldn't track down his hotel and it turned out that he didn't have one, he was hiding out at a "safe house" or something, so dasvidaniya to him.

There are exceptions to every rule; take the Pianist **Victor Borge**, for example. He was a staple on the Ed Sullivan show, and younger people may have seen him as a pie-in-the-face Comedian old fart, but get a whiff of this...long before there were Rockers that threw things from hotel windows (TV sets, burning mattresses, the hotel manager and staff) there I was, still a kid, watching ol' Victor on a film clip play a Classical piece, and for a flourish finale, he pushed the grand piano INTO THE HOTEL POOL; you could say he was ahead of his time.

BOBBY CURTOLA-

Him.

BMG had a Special Products division and his '**Hits**' package was one of them. Bobby was HUGE in the late 50's, early 60's, and Canadian too. He had hits like "**Indian Giver**" which wouldn't fly THESE days HOWEVER one has to recognize that he, **Paul Anka** and a VERY select one or two others made it BIG *without* the benefit of **Canadian Content** rules; the cream rose to the top.

My wife, Lynne was all excited about Bobby's music, and she told me how enraptured she was when she was at one of his shows when she was younger and he gave her his Coke bottle and what a treasure that was (gag). I remember **Margo Timmins** (**Cowboy Junkies**) telling me how one of HER treasures was the beer bottle **Lou Reed** gave her at one of his concerts; I'm sure there's a parallel there in some universe, but Lou made one of the **BEST** Rock Rcords ever with his "**Rock & Roll Animal**," and Bobby didn't.

Anyway, I gave Lynne a CD, but told her she could NEVER play it while I was in the house, seemed fair to me.

Bobby was a bubbly little guy and had an office near **CISL** in Richmond, and would drop in unannounced and pop on air, so I was careful to monitor the station as I was heading there for their sister station Z95. I heard him drop in on **Don Percy**, and he was all over Don like a wet shirt, especially about his upcoming tour sponsored by a vegetable juice company, which caused me to think, "hmmm. Given the median age of his fans, which would be 50 to Death, probably closer to Death, to make any money on this tour you'd have to do afternoon shows and sell Prune juice in Oxygen bars." They COULD have ramped up attendance by offering a door prize of one Motorized Potty/WheelChair, the snazzy **Lincoln Incontinental**! I continued to listen as Bobby was in full Gush over Don, but missed him when I finally got to the station, dang! I guess I just didn't want my hand licked.

Bobby at one time had a TV show; you know your recording career is in the ditch when TV asks you to do a show. The ONLY reason I tuned in was to see his guest, **Bo Diddley**! Well, Bo was as great as TV allowed him to be in those days, but at the end of the show Bo is on again, and in mid-song up pops Bobby; Bo is playing his axe and doing his shuffle, just *GIVIN'ER*, and Bobby is right there beside him trying to keep up, but you know, it was obvious to me that Bobby didn't know Diddly.

For the record, **Bo Diddley's** real name is **Elias McDaniel** and he used to make guitars from cigar boxes as a child and in Africa. An instrument like this is called a **diddley bow** (starting to GET it?); it's a "Roots" thing. He used to make posters for his tour dates that read: If you think Elvis is the King then you don't know Diddley! Love it.

CONAN DALY-

From BMG Calgary; one of the FUNNIEST men on 3 wheels! He and **Dale Peters** from Toronto were an ongoing **HOWL** at conventions, and Conan was a driven and dedicated music man

THE DAVE MATTHEWS BAND-

Took me FIVE years to break them on Vancouver Radio; **100.3TheQ/ Victoria** knew it all along! Once the light **DID** go on in YVR during my spot on **The Fox's Rep Report**, I had the opportunity to thank "the hundreds of thousands of Freeloading Bastards for stealing the band's latest record on-line," causing us to have them go back and do a NEWER version, which, well you know...sigh. We got **CALLS**! It was good radio.

Go to **Soundcloud** and check out the sound bite of the show, host **Jeff O'Neil**

https://soundcloud.com/user-467057850/ripping-them-a-new-one

L>R Dale Robertson/BMG, Dave Matthews/DMB, Skunkface Killah/Me, Terry Mulligan/TDM, Miss Katherine/BMG. Backstage at the Commodore. You may have seen this in Terry's book, I haven't.

Pulling The Fox's tail: The 1st time **Dave Matthews Band** played here it was at Vancouver's Bastion of the Counter Culture: **The Town Pump**. I'd seen them previously at a convention in Seattle and went away confused, as musically, the band and I didn't connect. *BUT* we had a record and it sounded pretty good, and now we had a live date and needed support. **The Q** was in, but we needed **The Fox** too. In spite of impressive American Radio activity, however, The Fox couldn't smell what we were cookin' and was holding its nose, saying it was 'too American', Huh? Like **Santana** maybe?

So, I coaxed, cajoled, begged and pleaded, all to no avail, annnnd here comes the band!

We had no airplay in Van, slow tix sales and a record and show to sell. We even went for the heart-strings (as well as the purse-strings) and involved the **Food Bank**.

Showtime! The venue is at least half empty (don't give me that 'glass of water' bullshit, I can count!) and I'm still from **Missouri** on the band, a couple songs in then, **BAM!** I got it! I'm enraptured and as I watch drummer **Carter Buford** (one of the **BEST** drummers I've ever experienced) I decide that when I die, I'm going to **HIS** house!

In spite of the low attendance, it was such a dynamic performance that, to hear people talk today, the band would have had to play the Coliseum to accommodate all the people that weren't actually there.

So, now truly inspired, I get home about 3AM and decide I **HAVE** to do something to show the strength of my conviction to get **The Fox's** attention, so, knowing nobody is actually there, I call the **PD** and say.".listen bud, Ray here, I just saw the **BEST** band I've **EVER** seen in my **LIFE** and if **The Fox** doesn't play the **Dave Matthews Band**, then **The Fox** is **F**KED!**."..then slam down the phone, which is only really effective to you, they only hear the click, but DAMN it feels good!

Next day, that message goes around **The Fox** offices, and in the Music meet to go thru every song on the LP and came up with Bupkiss! They just couldn't hear it!

So after 4 more YEARS of tilting at Windmills with The Fox and DMB, *their* light goes on, and now they knew it all along! God I hate my life.

Reco- Dave Matthew Band, "Don't Drink the Water," "Everyday"

JOHN DENVER-

A huge talent on stage and studio, great songwriter, polite, appreciative and remembered people well. A joy to work with. **"Leavin' on a Jet Plane"** too soon.

DIDO

Her simply brilliant *No Angel* album dropped upon us in May 1999, and remains one of the Best albums I've heard.

It was a giant priority for the U.S. (Arista) label and for us at BMG, in Canada, but I didn't need to be told that, as I could both hear and feel it from the grooves to my inner ear.

This was a time when relationships with Radio still counted and Radio still listened locally, altho hearing loss was fast upon them; they were spending kajillions to "test" and "research" music and were quickly painting themselves into a consulted corner.

Our Vancouver area Top 40 Titan was Z95, and Music Director (MD) Curtis Strange had great ears and an open mind. It was a time when you could "break" (get a record or artist started on air) without the benefit (?) of Radio Consultants that Radio had hired to counter the Independent Record Promoters used by big American labels, as many were considered to be corrupt (huh, maybe a pot/kettle thing?).

Most Radio Consultants didn't operate out of the cities in which they consulted.

So anyways...I was at home one evening watching TV with Lynne, one of her shows, *Roswell* (which was a huge hit), something I wouldn't normally watch at gunpoint, maybe I thought I'd get lucky...and I DID!

Thankfully, the show was ending and the credits and music rolled...WTF! The music was Dido's "Here with Me," the very song we had to break, and I had NO idea that it was the show's theme!

Straight out of bed the next morning I was on the phone to my Promo Domo in Toronto about the well-kept secret, and asked him in the nicest possible way **(*Wink!*)** if he *had* a moment to please get me the *Roswell* TV show demographics (viewers by age) from their Ad Agency and whisk it away to me **AT THE SPEED OF GODDAM LIGHT!**

"Here with Me" was bubbling up on American Radio and Trade Magazine airplay charts/ Bibles, but this activity notwithstanding, the Ad Agency Demographic info was the KEY to opening the door for us here in Canada, rather than sit around on our spotty behinds waiting for the Americans to do our jobs for us.

I brought the stats into Z95 at my next opportunity and put them in front of Curtis, saying "THIS is your station's audience!" He agreed, and started featuring the song for listener reaction back-selling the *Roswell* connection with it, and it grew from there!

I was SO excited at this breakthrough, I called Dido's Product Manager at Head Office. His response?

"It's about f@#*ing time!"

Par'Me?

Promo Monkey: My Life as a BellHop in the Waldorf Hysteria

Seriously?

Well, Fu*k *You* very much, I thought, and his words were the beginning of the idea for Early Retirement a couple years later; it may have hurt my pride but never killed my passion.

Ignoring ignorance, there were better things to come before I left, namely meeting Dido in person!

Nettwerk Management mega-mind Terry McBride had thankfully taken a local management position with Dido, which made media work ever so much easier; I knew him from other projects and welcomed it.

She did everything asked of her, including a live Radio interview at Z95 to cement the TV/Radio connection with fans and listeners, as well as charming media and retail store people at a special dinner, all the while being totally down to earth, a Goddess Godsend to work with.

Dido! Dido! It's off to work I go!!!!

This has been the Stan-less Steal Version

L>R: *Warren Copnick/Nat'l Promo Mgr BMG Canada, the Lovely Dido, Rob Mice PD Radio Z95, Myself/ Radio & Media Mgr BMG YVR at Pacific Coliseum Vancouver*

DOOMSBURY-

One time **RCA** released a **Doonesbury/Jimmy Thudpucker** LP that was tuneful enuff, but I felt it needed an obvious boost, so I contacted the Press Barons at The **Vancouver Sun** (Vancouver's Daily Planet) and spoke with somebody that sounded as tho they might just be Perry White (played by Ed Asner). What I wanted was to buy ad space in the comic section, where **Doonesbury** ran, for the LP, but his reaction was akin to my breaking ALL Ten Commandments at once, and I was put on notice, Record Company conniving sniveler that I was esteemed to be, that in **NO** way would they sell ad space in **that** section, it was considered taking advantage of a somewhat captive audience/readership! Uh huh, and...RATS! Thwarted again! Having said that, it comes to mind that once you couldn't buy the front page either, but today, if you want to read page one, you have to look inside the Ad wrapper the papers come in, which serves as the cover, huh.

DOUG & THE SLUGS-

Had a hand in signing them too, great act, successful records. Enjoyed "Slugging" it out. Sam & Denise were a great team to tag with.

Small world, turns out my neighbor in the steaming metropolis of Ladner, **Ted Laturnas,** was one of Doug's original drummers.

Doug & Slugs celebrating their 1st Gold Album (*Cognac and Bologna*) in fine Bennett fettle at the stately Bayshore Inn. But seriously folks, that's **SUGAR** not 'the real thing' and no Burton of proof to the contrary!

...and then, years later...this

It was one Heck of an event!

Bill Henderson's "Cover me with Roses" at Doug's Celebration of Life at The Commodore just floored me, still does.

Too Bad, indeed.

"...just let me finish..."

Douglas Craig Bennett
October 31, 1951 –
October 16, 2004

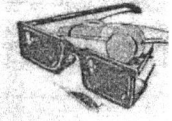

Remembered with love; Nancy, Della, Shea and Devon

ELVIS-

He up and died the day I was hired at **RCA** (I had nothing to do with that, **NOTHING!**) and, not to be outdone, **Bing Crosby** died about a month later. So, I never met the man, but I DID get to see the top of Priscilla's hairdo one day when I was in Vegas for an Elvis Convention, and I did get to say "hi" to The Colonel (Parker, not Saunders, altho he WAS licking his fingers) who was sitting beside his new protégé, **Rick Nelson**, signing autographs. Fortunately for him, he didn't have his "Dancing Chickens" show with him, or the **ASPCA** would have shut the entire thing down. Carnies...sigh.

Elvis imitators? Should get a life, preferably one of their own. That's just spooky.

One time, **John Ford** and I were in LA and went to the legendary "**Palomino Club**," a Country Music venue (we knew we were getting closer to the Club by the increasing amount of cars up on blocks). That night they were hosting an **Elvis** night, and one of the performers was a Black guy in a white jump suit, the whole bit. He was just givin' it, but there were some ring-ass Rednecks in the room and they were not encouraging him, so we left before things could escalate into a **race** riot before the Triple K (**KKK**) Ball team arrived. But they MISSED the point: Here was a Black man doing Elvis, and all Elvis really was, was a White cracker doing a Black man.

L>R: *The Late Leagh Alden/RCA, the Right on time Myself, and Red Robinson; presenting Red with Double Platinum for his contribution to the '***Elvis: Canadian Tribute** *project. Without Red there wouldn't have been that album; AGAIN! No Red, No Elvis!*

"ENTERTAINMENT CONSULTANT"-

I made this up and have NO idea what it might mean. I put it on my Biz Card so people would ask and we'd start talking. This sounded better than my original title of "Grizzly Promotions," a play on the Grizzly Ramsay nickname, but that sounded like I specialized in bear maulings and shark attacks, so I changed it.

Ray Ramsay / Entertainment Consultant

www.aladinladner.simplesite.com

grizzlyramsay@telus.net

Rockin' the WRock, White Rock BC Canada

Hums, TALL Tales & Short Stories

I have known and worked with a number of Consultants; most are a credit to their craft (**Pat Bohn**'s crew were my favorite), but some are a joke. At one convention, we had one person in particular, I'll just call him Mr. Smartass, and we actually PAID this guy to tell us things *I* had some better answers for and *then* he had the nerve to tell all of us we looked like we read books! **Gasp! Oh NO!** Something really has to be done about this literacy problem! I bet the last book this guy read had word balloons or boobs in it! And THEN, we fed this jackass lunch! I waited around to see if he'd choke, but no luck

Meet **Jim JJ Johnston**, Consultant Extraordinaire! I met JJ when he came West in the mid 1980's to helm what was then CHR Powerhouse **CKLG73**, and we had fun!

He is now, and has been for some time a Consultant that still loves Radio and the industry at large, and is active on **FaceBook/FYI Music** with his **JJ 365** posting of what he terms the Good Ones. By doing this puts a more human face on people from the Record/Music Industry, which may be seen by outsiders as a bunch of kidnappers, tramps and thieves (no matter

HOW we disguise it). Jim was a gas to work with, and that's no reference to the bean salads we'd consume over lunch noshes!

JJ has a great sense of humor, but is also a deep thinker when planning things, and once shared a bit of philosophy that's stayed with to this day, sage advice.

Along with Mike Pleau's breakthrough, the John Farnham single "You're the Voice" (see "Mike Pleau: Little Big Man" in *Promo Monkey; Monkey See, Monkey TWO*), JJ's adding the track sent the "Voice" echoing across Canada!

Reco- John Farnham, "You're the Voice"

The album (google it) soared past the gold mark (50,000) sales in Canada as a result. He added the "**Age of Reason**" as the second track to reinforce the artist to their listeners. Also on the LP was a version of AC/DC's, Farnham's fellow Aussies, "**It's a Long way to the Top**," here's the video….

Reco- John Farnham, "Long Way to the Top Pop Version (Live)" YouTube

CHATTER #5

*Pre-Stunt: (From Left) Leagh Alden/RCA, Me Truly/RCA,
Little Orphan Annie Lennox (Sort of)
Photo courtesy of RayMan Ramsay, Shooter Bev Shannon-Friesen*

EURYTHMICS-

Great music, odd people. I pulled off an odd promo for their "**Touch**" album by dressing up a clothing mannequin as Annie, with bright orange hair and in a man's suit, notified the media, especially the Traffic departments of Radio Stations, about a possible traffic jam in front of **A&B Sound** one afternoon due to the "principals" of a **Eurythmics** promotion arriving, which was me, Bev, and "Annie" arriving in a limo to complete a window display. Got a LOT of coverage out of **THAT** one!

As there was still time on the meter, after that, Bev and I took the limo, **Union Jacks** flapping, to **White Spot** for burgers, and by the time we arrived at the Marine Drive location, we were wearing our Black masks like Annie on the *Touch* cover. The Car-Hops couldn't figure out who we were and we were howling with laughter, so they probably thought we were high. We weren't "Tall" at all, we were HUNGRY; OH, the stuff we used to do.

Another time I was convinced that by placing their LP graphic UPSIDE DOWN in an **A&B Sound** print ad we'd have a good part of the town flipping their papers over to see what it was, piquing the curiosity of onlookers. After much shouting back & forth with the buyer, I won out, and the record sold like **CRAZY**. This was something that I heard Guinness did in England when sales were down; Libate and learn.

I once met them at the airport and they were hard to miss; Annie was wearing a striped 1920's full body bathing suit and Dave was looking VERY colourful and like he had been pulled thru a hedge backward.

EVERLAST-

His **"Whitey Ford Sings the Blues"** joint was a Rap/Rock Hybrid and the **"What It's Like"** track, a natural hit. **The Fox** was smitten, and in a conversation with Bob and Rob, I happened to mention that while we'd had records on The Fox chart, I'd never had a **#1** on it. Then, on Feb 22/99, two unique things happened:

1. The **Everlast** CD went to #1 on The Fox chart, and...

2. The Fox presented ME (Not BMG) with a #1 Plaque!

This NEVER happens; it's ALWAYS the rep or label giving Radio the plaque, but there it hangs in the Ramseum in our house, and I'm STILL flattered to this day, Everlasting.

*The FOX Vancouver's **Rob Robson** and **Bob Mills** gave BMG Canada promo rep Ray Ramsay this plaque commemorating his first #1 record at the station after more than 20 years of servicing it. Everlast's* What It's Like *was the track that broke the streak.*

THE FABS-

Never met **The Beatles,** but did meet John's son **Julian,** (the inspiration for "**Hey Jude**"); nice, grounded lad. Also knew one of their former "Advance Men", **Liam Mullen,** who once worked for **Brian Epstein**. Handled two of **Ringo's** records at **RCA 'Old Wave'** and *Stop & Smell the Roses* one was considered so bad by other territories/markets and labels, it was only released in Canada and Germany. Maybe they should have called the latter "Stop & Smell the Vodka"; they were more Drinko than Ringo, too bad. He also had a later record out on **Private Music,** but Radio didn't go near it.

I'm an avid reader and have my own library, but had to ask my family & friends to stop giving me books about the **Beatles,** as I now know more about them than their parents did.

I drew this so many years from now, but it just seems like Yesterday, to me
Beatles toon/tune by yers truly

SAM FELDMAN-

Got **Doug and the Slugs** for **RCA**. Someone whose name rhymes with 'Bruce' said that any label that would sign **Nestor Pistor** would sign these guys, and he was RIGHT! Sam hung on for the ride of his life; a Gentleman and a Professional, AND a nice guy to boot!

Sam and Bruce

These guys have a Right to their Opinion and a pretty good left too!

FERGIE-

Was with the female vocal group "**Wild Orchid**" when they were on **RCA** and were the opening act for Cher/Cyndi Lauper's "Middle-Age Girls Just Wanna Have Fun Too" tour during its Vancouver stop. There wasn't a lot to say, as their single hadn't yet clicked, altho I had arranged some "feature" play on one of the Top 40 Stations. Eventually the record was a miss and **Wild Orchid** withered. **Fergie** went on to become one of the **Black-Eyed Peas**; no idea what happened to the other two, but I bet they aren't wild about orchids!

FINTRY QUEEN-

An old paddle-wheel boat on Okanagan Lake/Kelowna that we rented for a night at an **RCA** Convention and then drank dry; the bar on the boat, not the lake. We was THIRSTY!

FLEETWOOD MAC-

Never had the pleasure **BUT**, while I was with **Quality,** an album came my way called "**Buckingham Nicks**" which lit me right up! "Here I go again." I shouted this from the rooftops. Nobody listened, **nobody**.

This was while **Fleetwood Mac** were still an English Blues band. Eventually, Lindsey and Stevie were invited to join them, which transformed them and the current Music world; after that, the "*Rumors*" were true!

Reco- Buckingham Nicks' entire first (and only) album- YouTube

JOHN FORD-

Who also came from **TPC/Quality** and hired me for **RCA Vancouver** the same day **Elvis** dropped freakin' dead (something I said?); an auspicious start. He was a friend, Manager and Mentor and is now happily playing golf on the Sunshine Coast. He deserves it; from Cowtown to MyTown to the Big Pineapple (T.O.) to the BIG Apple and back, quite a ride!

His 50th Birthday

Quite a Soiree at his house. Friends, family, and loads of Music Industry Nabobs.

I made him a card. **Bruce Allen** came by with Seafood, yay Bruce, fresh Crab!

Possibly TOO fresh.

Things were going swimmingly until my wife noticed some movement on the Crab table; they were still ALIVE, and LEAVING! Forget the BIRTHDAY party, they were gonna bust a move and have a BREAKOUT party, aaaaand they're OFF!

…and here's a roomful of panicked, screaming people trying to head them off and grab them and getting into an, ummmm PINCH for their trouble. Don't do that.

So, Lynne, being a Fisherman's Daughter, calmly grabbed them by their hairy behinds, and 'potted' them, 'containing' the situation.

Remember: **NEVER** try to pick up a Crab from the **FRONT**, *that's* the business end of the beast, the pointy, painful part. Reach *around* and pick them up by the back porch, *that's* the painless part.

After all, they are called Crabs for a reason.

John Ford caricature 50th Birthday card by Ray Ramsay

JIM FOSTER-

Yes, he of the Vancouver Rockhaus band **Fosterchild**. Had the pleasure of working with him during his RCA album **Power Lines** which included their opening slot for the red-hot **Mr. Mister** dates in Kelowna and YVR @ the Queen E.

Good guys, Good band, still friends.

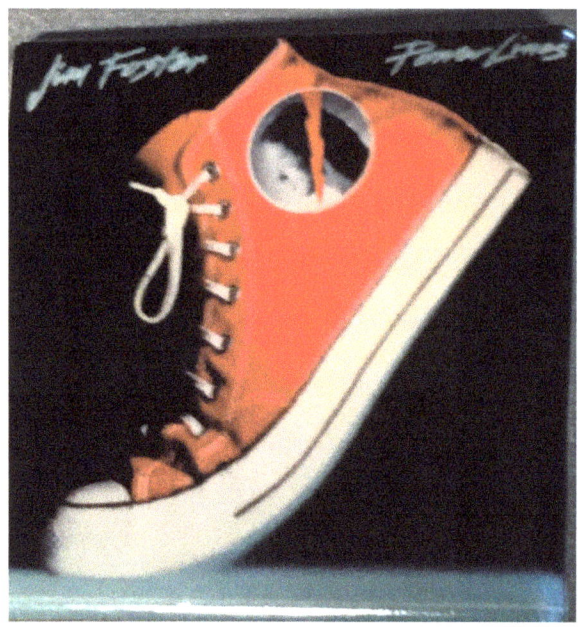

RADNEY FOSTER-

I LOVE a good scrap! Davy Crockett said "Make sure you're right, then go ahead." Good advice that didn't turn out so well for him, BUT...Radney had a record, and the record was Hot, BUT the local Country Station didn't believe in it until we had **Radney** in town for a showcase and I put the shoe on the other hoof between the **MD** and him, then **BAM!** We won. The record was called "**Nobody Wins**"; not true!

He is a great guy, an equally great writer (ask the Dixie **Chicks**) and a fine fellow to work with.

Reco- Radney Foster, "Don't Say Goodbye"

CHATTER #6

THE GRAMMYS/1985-

I think I'm the first person from the **Queen Charlotte Islands** to go to the **Grammys**; I know someone else has gone since, a young lady, I think. The Grammys are still the Grammys but the **QCI** are now **Haida Gwaii**. I was born there.

So *anyways*, this all happened because the **Jefferson Starship** didn't. That is to say, they had the biggest hit song ("**We Built This City**") in the free world and were unable to sell out the 2800 seats in the **Queen Elizabeth Theatre**! This was from a new LP, which I recall **Tom Harrison** (*The Province*) reviewing and giving four dollar signs ($$$$) instead of stars. The review consisted of him saying "Who *ARE* these people?!" What a riot!

Ticket sales were lacking, but record sales weren't, and at that point we had Gold Award plaques for them, but with them gone, Bryan Boyce, the Branch Manager and I were summoned to LA by our own **John Ford** (in New York at that time) to present the **Canadian Gold** to the band at The Grammys! Whoo Hoo! NOW we had to be fitted for Tuxes, get ticketed and get GOING!

First, we stood in the Forever Line at customs clutching the Plaques; then, once we got thru with minutes to spare, we were sent to the WRONG boarding gate at the OTHER end of the airport and had to create our own chase scene to get to the right one where they were holding the plane for us. Once on board, we had to pass **Bryan Adams and Bruce Allen**, who were howling at these antics, OH the shame.

Now at LAX we had a limo pick us up and went straight to the Marmont, which was so posh I think we took our shoes off to go inside, where we were told we had to wear shoes.

It was a nice thought, but putting me up in a Classy joint like that was a bit like giving Ice Cream to Pigs; it's all slop to a hog, and I was used to humbler digs, but there I was!

I was used to staying at the **Hollywood Hyatt**, known in the Music Biz as the **Hollywood RIOTT**; at home there's highway signs warning about falling rocks? At the **Riott** they have signs that warn "**Watch for falling Rockers**". Yeah.

So, we're at this classy hotel and go to the rooftop patio, where we were greeted with the vision of a topless Top Heavy Sunbathing Beauty; so what do you say? Hello! Nice to meet the both of you! Then, with the visage of the **Grand Tetons** fresh in our minds, we quick did a Tux up, and went off to meet John and limo it to the **Shrine Auditorium**; heady stuff.

It was a GREAT show of course, but leaving the Shrine we were beset by a horde of rather keen young ladies in search of autographs; they swarmed us, asking "are you FAMOUS?, Well, no but" …FOOM! Gone!

Then, off we went to the label reception to present former Acid Casualties with gold plaques from Canada, schmooze with stars, and drink deeply, then fall into a DEEP sleep back at the hotel.

The two things I remember about the next morning are ordering breakfast and my eggs "over,'" and the waiter, somewhat exasperated, asking, "Over, how?!" Me: over on the OTHER side! THEN, meeting **Jose Menendez**, then Head of **RCA**, and obviously before Lyle and Eric turned on him and Kitty and he became the Late… Nice guy, very gracious.

Apparently, his sons Lyle and Eric shot them both so they could get their Life Insurance money and open a restaurant, but "We were hungry" hardly equals Justifiable Homicide, and now they have life-long records of their own.

A bit later, it's time to leave, and Oh My, how times have changed! No limo now, we're given a taxi (possibly because the Gardeners had taken all the wheel barrows). On the way to LAX I had a first-hand experience with near-death experiences in LA, as I saw a guy with a camera crossing the road near us be **NAILED** by a car, **NAILED!** He went Ass over Tea Kettle thru the air then got up and walked away! So, this cameraman had a second job as a stuntman?!

Just crossing the street can be life threatening down there; first the drug dealers and bangers follow you slowly in their cars as you walk down the street until they're satisfied you're not a cop, THEN they *consider* letting you cross. Pedestrians **DO NOT** have the right of way; they have the right of flight.

A few years ago, David Foster ran over Chicken George (Ben Vereen) as he crossed the road (raising an age-old question) in the dark. So, if a **BIG**, bright star like **THAT** can be run down, what chance do we have?

HollyWeird, really.

Canadian Gold to Jefferson Starship backstage at the Grammys (L>R) Starship members (3) John Ford- RCA US Director, Me- RCA Canada, Bryan Boyce- RCA Canada, Grace Slick (are those Pajamas?), Elliot Goldman- Head Mucky-Muck RCA U.S., more band guys, the Late Jose Menendez (now, not then)- RCA Exec VP RCA U.S., Bill Thompson/Mgr Jefferson Starship and Main Hanger occupant.

CHATTER #7

DAVID GRAY, "WHITE LADDER"-

WHAT a story! A Career project.

Thank GOD for **100.3 TheQ**!

Thank God for **CTV!**

Built this one from the ground up; everybody at our branch just BELIEVED. I went about the Media, approaching empathetic Musically Intelligent people to pitch David as Van Morrison for the New Millennium (altho NOBODY can stand in that man's shoes, nobody), and slowly they opened up and came on board. That is to say, Print and TV, Radio in Vancouver had **NO** interest in this **AT ALL** *at that time*. We were on Full Ignore. However, the good people at **TheQ / Victoria**, who had open minds and ears, were on this like a wet shirt, as was **Peter Grainger at CTV,** who is an avid Music fan. He sensed a story developing here and gave us coverage galore, including an interview and Gold Record presentation to **TheQ/Al Ford**.

David was coming to The Commodore and the show sold out in moments! As The Q had supported us SO well, I asked the promoters, **House of Blues**, if they could have the "Presents" for image if nothing else, and they granted it. Altho The Q was Vancouver's worst kept secret, this was their coming out and it went VERY well, and I'm proud to have had a hand in that.

John Shields at The Q was thrilled with the coverage his station got from the effort. Here's a clip from his email to me: "The coverage was beyond my wildest expectations. I know there are some who think of you as a gruff, cantankerous, foul-mouthed son of a Bitch! And you know what? I'm one of them. It's an endearing quality. But you also must know that in my estimation, there are no other people in the record business who has the passion, tenacity and energy, to get things done like you." There's more but that's enuff, I'm getting teary.

In the end, it comes down to sales for a label, and here I go being proud again, but the "**White Ladder**" record went **Gold** (at that time), and **80%** of Canada's sales were in BC, and 80% of those were split between Vancouver and Victoria, without one second's airplay in Vancouver!

If you don't try, you don't do.

Givin' the GOLD! 14 Carat to 100.3! https://youtu.be/cBA7xzQbvBw

Reco- David Gray, "Say Hello, Wave Goodbye"

BUDDY GUY-

What a player! What a project; I had to **FIGHT** for this one, but when the going gets tough…the tough get Gold Records!

This involved **Buddy (with Jeff Beck)** doing the R&B Classic "**Mustang Sally**" at the same time 1991 ("***Damn Right I Got the Blues***" LP) as the non-band "**The Commitments**" from the movie of the same name, not quite "The Archies" but…

HALL & OATES-

Sara smiled for a while, until she heard "**Voices**," which shipped Gold and came back the same way, then suddenly, **BAM!** Couldn't press enough fast enough. Very professional to work with. A hilite of one visit here was them being interviewed by **Terry Mulligan**; they told him after it was the

BEST interview they'd ever done! Their success was assured at that point. **Diddy Do Wop**, indeed. They even nicked The Fabs on "**How does It Feel to Be Back**."

Reco- Hall & Oates- "How Does It Feel To Be Back," "Diddy Doo Wop (I Hear the Voices)"

EMMY-LOU HARRIS-

If Honey had a voice, it would be hers.

HATS-

Can reveal a person's musical inclination. For example: Peak to the back= Rap, Peak to the front= Rope (Country), Peak sideways= Agnostic, or simply dressed in the dark.

Rap (Hip Hop) and Rope (Heck Hop) are Polar opposites; a Country group tried Country Rap, but I think the people caught them and tossed them into a Hay Baler, yeah.

THE HIGGINS-

A Post-Raytirement (meaning I can't leave well enough alone) project. I stumbled across them one Sunday at one of the **Ladner Market Days**, as I saw my old friend **David Wills (Stonebolt)** with them. Nice bunch of kids. David told me they were going to be recording an album, writing some stuff themselves, and in the front of my mind was this **Patty Griffin** track that the **Dixie Chicks** missed called "**Useless Desires**," so I told David about it and got the group some copies for consideration.

Reco- Patty Griffin, "Useless Desires", "Florida"

I was not working for anyone's interest at this point; it's just a good, if not great, song.

A while later, David calls and asks me to come to **SoundKitchen Studios** to hear something, which was THE song, demoed by The Higgins. A chill went up my spine; a good sign. Dollar signs are better, but…

I was doing some charity work later on for the **Delta Hospital's "Light the way" Campaign** to raise money for the hospital and got **The Higgins** the entertainment slot (and the publicity that went with that). They played the track in their set, I got 'nother chill and NOT from the weather. But in the end, it didn't make the album; out of our hands and too bad, as that song may have opened doors for their own songs later. I still think it could for somebody.

BRUCE HORNSBY-

Spiderfingers to some, Bruce *Jazzby* to me, for his freestyle keyboards.

He came to us at RCA in 1986 with his epic debut album, "The Way It Is," with his band, The Range. They went from Rock FM to the top of the Top 40, a dazzling introduction, much like the playing.

I worked with him a few times in various configurations of bands, and it was always a good experience. The most memorable was the first time he appeared in YVR (Pacific Coliseum) opening for his benefactor Huey Lewis (and the News); an auspicious debut here, indeed. It was his Huey-ness that took it on himself to assail all and sundry in the Biz that they shud sign "The Range" (as they were then known) or else! And Nipper heard him…*who's* a good dog?!

The date was very timely, as Bruce's album had just gone Canadian Gold (50,000+ sales), and I had the great pleasure of not only presenting Bruce with a Gold award, but also Huey!

Gold Caps for Bruce and Huey. L>R Dale Buote Radio CFMI, currently Rock101,

King Midas du jour- Me, Bruce Hornsby, Huey Lewis, going for the Golden Touch!

Shooter-Joness Bowie

Later on in my Romp & Roll thru the Music Biz, the **Dave Matthews Band** came along, and I found that Dave hailed from Virginia just like Bruce. Two intensely creative people from the same area, and we deserved them both.

Bruce has had a long and varied career; he's even been Dead, in a nice manner of speaking.

For all things Hornsby, peep www.brucehornsby.com. That's the way it is!

WHITNEY HOUSTON-

I met her before her star had fully risen, before the hits, and before she became Bobby Brown's punching bag. She was nice, if aloof.

Her first hit broke locally on **CFMI**, pre-**Rock 101** days, **not** Top 40.

We met up a few more times, once at a BMG Convention where we did an entire BMG staff and Whitney photo, kind of a "Where's Waldo" Sardine can photo, and once again in Vancouver, where the big thrill for me was meeting her Mom, **Cissy Houston**.

Cissy was part of "**The Sweet Inspirations**" who recorded for Atlantic in their Soul days and made some pretty fine records. They also backed Elvis on a tune or two; it was a thrill and she was sweet.

L>R: Whitney in happier times with Marty Forbes PD/97 Kiss, and Me, with what looks like Gas.
Photo by Joness Bowie

HUDSON BROTHERS-

Brett, Mark & Bill of the **Keenan Wynn** clan, from **Everyday Hudson** to seizing the spotlight. They had a summer replacement TV variety show and a hit single, "**So You Are a Star**," from their debut LP on **Casablanca**. I gave this project my everything, but didn't even get a thank you, but I did get shit on; thanks **Bill**, the pressure was all mine.

To make matters worse, the album they were recording while they were in Vancouver came out on another label, **MCA**. I did have a record to sell, but there was NO future in it.

TERRY JACKS-

Which way you goin', Terry?

Up, fishing, to the Bank, you pick.

Worked with him when I was with TPC/**Quality**. He had a single, "**Christine**," which did well. I remember taking an acetate of the track to his house in Horseshoe Bay and being blown away when I saw he had a brook, a BROOK! Running thru his living room, and all this BEFORE he had his Season in the Sun!

ALAN JACKSON-

A good guy, talented writer, **nobody** here would play his first single "**Blue-Blooded Woman (and a Red Neck Man)**" now…

The first time I met Alan, he was opening for **Randy Travis**, who was sober and had his clothes on at the time, at the **Coliseum/PNE**, which had a dress code. Alan was a bit nervous, but very gracious, and did everything he was asked.

Yours truly with Alan Jackson, one the BEST Country singers and writers, ever. Photo by Dee Lippingwell.

Reco- Alan Jackson, "He Stopped Loving Her Today," "Drive," "It's 5 o' Clock Somewhere" with Jimmy Buffet

JAKE-

A Post-Raytirement project.

"Jake" is actually John, husband of my **BMG** Bud **Val Lapp**, AND is a "Kids" project; hard to promote, but not impossible! She contacted me to do some work on this.

Our first meeting was at a McDonald's next to the play area, fittingly enough. To make this work, I NEEDED something to hang my hat on, and TELUS had great success with "**Hippopotamus for Christmas**," and I found "**Underpants in Hawaii**" (a good fit!) on Jake's new CD, so off I went. Hmmm…a 'Hippo' in 'My Underpants'…could be Big!…in a nice manner of speaking.

I hit on EVERYBODY, *especially* Radio Morning shows, got a lot of awareness, gained some exposure, including a solid TV op, and some gigs! Later that year, "**Jake**" was nominated for a **JUNO Award**! Don't know what or even IF I had anything to do with that, but it felt good regardless.

I recall picking Val up at the ferry and racing to YVR so she could catch her flight to Toronto for the Awards with a trunk full of ladies' dresses and stuff from the store my wife, Lynne, was working at. Once at the airport, Val went thru the trunk in the parking lot, took some nice new stuff for the Awards, and then OFF she flew! Talk about full-service support.

Sadly, but not unexpectedly, the sale of the clothing was totally lost on the store owners; THEIR clothing brand was going to the Junos, maybe even on camera! Nothing. Their clothing chain is closed now, SURPRISE! The power of positive shirking. You just can't help some people.

CHATTER #8

COLIN JAMES-

I never worked with him, and possibly haven't met him, altho that would be strange for the Vancouver Music Biz, as everyone was orbiting in and out of each other's space, and Colin is a fixture of the scene.

I do know, and have worked with, his more-than-capable Manager, **Paul Mercs**, over the years, so he's been in good hands; the torch was eventually passed to the likewise capable **Mary Levitan**.

Paul had a strong support staff that included the inimitable **Deb Macko** and future media star **Tamara Taggart**, who would eventually drop anchor with **CTV News** in Vancouver.

I remember a story from when he was just breaking out as a Blues player and they tried to book him dates in American Blues clubs with limited success, the reason being that while he had the *chops* and the *sound*, he didn't have the **LOOK**, which is to say he wasn't old, downtrodden and beaten up with his nose sniffing one ear, and he was WHITE. But, trouper that he is, he overcame all that.

There was a time when it seemed Vancouver was awash in Blues (Jim **Byrnes, Colin, the Powder Blues Band, Uncle Wiggly's Hot Shoes Blues Band** etc.), and it may have affected tourism (Dude, don't go there, they're all a depressed, glum lot, y'know?) in the same way **Stephen King** may have affected tourism in the state of **Maine** (Man! Don't GO there! It's all Vampires and Monsters and shit!)

BOB JAMIESON-

A GREAT guy, REAL character, and he brought **BMG Canada** out of the Dork Ages. **ANY** President of a label that would dress up as **ZZ Top** and go out in public to promote their new record is just Jake with me. LOVE you JBob, wherever you are!

(L>R) The (Late) Rudi Gasner CEO of BMG Int'l, Carole Wright-VP BMG Canada, (She could skate circles around a LOT of Record people, really!) the One & Only Bob Jamieson-Pres of BMG Canada, Rs truly with BMG Canada's first Promo Rep of the Year Award (well-deserved but I've NO idea what that shit is coming out of my pocket), My Boss, Larry (Lawrence-of-a-Radio) MacRae-Nat'l Promo BMG Canada, Stormin' Norman Miller-Product Mgr & owner of the LOUDEST shirt in the photo- BMG Canada, Tim Williams-Sales Mgr and guy trying to whistle up a drink cuz this is taking too long-BMG Canada, and next to Bob, wearing the most somber suit in the room.

JEFF HEALEY BAND-

Jeff was a talented guitar stylist, a real nice guy and held it all together. As a group, it was the Blind leading the Bland.

JINGLE CATS-

Sorry, but I had a job to do. In the Music Biz, they don't pay you to **Like** them, they pay you to **SELL** them. Ditto **Jingle Dogs**, sigh.

BILLY JOEL-

His **FIRST** LP *Cold Spring Harbor* got him on the air, and away he went to **CBS**, probably owns his own harbour now.

SIR ELTON JOHN-

He wasn't "Sir" when I met him, but he was a bit surly. Then, he was just Reg Dwight hiding in plain sight. **Quality** had the **Paramount** Soundtrack to the *Friends* movie, which Elton had done the music for, and I think he wanted to distance himself from that, altho it was a darn good album. I was at a reception for him in Vancouver, prior to his sold-out concert at the Coliseum. I met a five foot nothing, partially balding gent with wings on his shoes, leading me to believe he and **KISS** shopped at the same store.

I shook what I thought was his hand, altho if you told me it was a damp dishrag, I would have believed you. I thought to myself, THIS is the guy that's going to blow the roof off the Coliseum tonight?!

It was and he did.

I should note that this didn't cool my enthusiasm for his music; one of the best tracks **EVER** done is his "**Skyline Pigeon**."

Reco- Elton John, "Skyline Pigeon" YouTube

CAROLYN DAWN JOHNSON-

WONDERFUL! WHAT a sweetheart! Beauty and Brains.

Promo Monkey: My Life as a BellHop in the Waldorf Hysteria

Thanks for helping **X91 Three** make **Carolyn Dawn Johnson** the **first Canadian artist** to have a **debut single hit number one** in **Canada**! **BMG Canada**'s **Ray Ramsay** presents **X 91 Three** Music Director **Scott James** and Senior Programming Manager **John Shields** with a **commemorative plaque** to mark the occasion.

X91.3 is gone, but The Zone carries on!

Reco-Carolyn Dawn Johnson, "Die of a Broken Heart"

Tom Jones-

If you googled Cool/Professional, his picture would pop up. A **REAL** pleasure.

His second career **Blues/Gospel** albums are a MUST to hear and have!

Reco- Tom Jones, "Dimming of the Day"

THE JUDDS-

Wynonna and **Naomi**. Sometimes laughing/lovingly referred to as Wyoming and Nairobi. Great act and sweethearts (of the Radio) as people.

Total professionals; I took Lynne with me to meet them backstage once, and two years later and after God knows how many other names and faces, we went back again and they greeted her by name, without any re-introduction! They remembered me too, but I'm just saying...

I recall once during a National Promo meeting we were going around the table checking the progress of some records on the Radio when their "**Grandpa**" deck was out, and one young rep burst forth with "...Come *on*! WHO cares about a Grandpa anymore!" marking a milestone in the breakdown of the Family unit. I thought, well *I* do, what are you, a lizard that came from an egg? You don't have to **like** them but you *DO* have to **sell** them, dude.

That's Me in the middle of a Meet sandwich with The Judds.
They were wonderful.(Joness Bowie Photo-1986)

Reco- The Judds, "Why Not Me," "Love Can Build a Bridge," "Mama He's Crazy,"

"Grandpa (Tell Me 'Bout The Good Old Days)"

THE JUNO AWARDS-

I've been to a few.

The ones out of town, **Toronto** for example, are generally exhausting affairs, as labels tend to attach all-day marathon meetings and aptitude courses (such as "how to negotiate your way out of a wet paper bag") that start a good THREE HOURS before you're even awake back at home, and THEN, guess what? You get a tour of bad nightclubs where your feet stick to the floors to hear bands make sounds not found in nature, *and* the next morning you're all eyeballs and assholes and not even sure which way is up, you're so tired. It's like being a **BellHop in the Waldorf Hysteria…hmmmm**

The awards show I recall the most was in **Vancouver at GM Place**, now **Rogers** Arena, as the GM lease lapsed and Jesus Chrysler Arena just didn't sound right.

So, this was the time our **Rascalz** won the **Rap Group** award and they refused to accept it, as its presentation had been marginalized by being presented off screen, and they felt both they and Rap in general had been dissed, and it had.

Case in point: retail sales charts being carried in trade publications eventually switched over from the "Honor System" (cough!) reports from stores to the **Soundscan** system, which required sales to be quantified by being scanned thru a till as an actual customer sale. Soon, a startling thing happened that put the lie to the old method: the **Top Sellers** were **Rap**, Country, and Soundtracks; **Rock** sales sank like one, the polar opposite of what once was. Mind you it, took about 10 minutes for some people to figure out a way to scam the scans but it was expen$ive…sigh.

So, the **Rascalz** were right, and good for them for taking a stand.

But then there was a problem, a logistical problem: award winners are normally escorted from the stage to the Media Room for their post-win reactions and pics, but **Rascalz** were there in the audience with us and had no way to get back!

BMG Canada Pres Lisa Zbitnew turned to me and asked if I could help; when the First Lady asks, you just DO it.

None of us had any accreditation to get backstage to the Media Room, especially me, the **Fearless Leader, BUT** I did what I've always done; take the Mental and Physical attitude that THIS is MY place, and it would be unwise to stop me; I belong! Sometimes, attitude is EVERYTHING!

So, that bit of cheek got us all though the various levels and **ALL** security, unquestioned, to the **Media Room**. Once I had **Rascalz** installed and saw they were **ok** with some of the BMG Press people that *were* there with credentials, I was approached by a Seer-Sucker Suited Security Staffer who asked to see my credentials. "Sorry, I don't have any, but as my job is done, I'm on my way, don't bother seeing me out, I know the way," and was off. I make new friends everywhere I go.

CHATTER #9

LEMMY KILMISTER (MOTÖRHEAD)-

For assuring me he could spell, who knew?

GENE KINISKI-

Canada's Greatest Athlete (because he said so) and **World Heavyweight Wrestling Champion** who returned my call (There's a Steve Lapinski on the phone for you!) to beg off being a participant in my **"Worlds Heavyweight Perogy Eating Contest"** with **Nestor Pistor** and other Media types (he doesn't eat before fights). This prompted me to ask him who Canada's **SECOND** Greatest Athlete was, hello? He was my hero, though.

KI$$-

Busted my BALLS for these guys. They were thrown out of Rock Radio repeatedly, but I finally got them on Top 40 using jukebox stats! I did everything in my power for this act and all I got was kicked in the same place I busted.

I was always found it interesting that they would use the Thunderbolt "S"s in their logo, as these guys are Jewish and those "S"s raises the specter of the Nasties from WW2, and all the shit that they did. The origin of the

Thunderbolt "S" comes from Scandinavia and was designated as the "Sig" sign many years before it became the Sig in "Sieg Heil!" and Sig-nister.

Gene is not a stupid man; **KISS** is a cash cow and always was; they were heavy into merchandising before a lot of other people caught on to it, so the Thunderbolt "S"s didn't Rune it, they made them richer.

In **Germany**, however, KISS is not allowed to use its trademark logo; they have to go with the conventional "**S**", Ghosts of Holocausts past and all, and this applies to their album graphics as well as on stage signage and lighting.

My final involvement with them was a concert at **The Coliseum**, which was a big deal, but **Quality** was strangely low profile on this. I went to the concert, and after some effort got backstage to meet the band, who, to a man, ignored me. Very confusing, until I bumped into the **Polygram** Rep who asked what I was doing there and told me KISS had signed with their **Mercury** label (in an effort to bankrupt them) that afternoon; somebody might have had the courtesy......

The silver lining is that I got to see the opening act **Cheap Trick,** which was MORE relatable to me, not being a 12 year-old any longer, and the only prop I saw was **Bun E. Carlos** oversized drumsticks

Pyrotechnics aside, in my opinion, **KISS** lights up a room when they *leave* it.

AVRIL LAVIGNE-

My last BIG act. From her 1st gig at the Electronic Arts cafeteria to her FREE show @ The Commodore, then on to GM Place, it was a trip. Had to trick her into talking with me by showing her a pic of my dog, otherwise, it was just a car ride with Grampa.

Avril was a bit of a handful, but was flush with success after the Free For All-Ages (for real) show we put on at **The Commodore** in conjunction with those great people at the **House of Blues** (now **LiveNation**), **Z95**,

Terry McBride at **Nettwerk Management,** and **BMG**. I did get rather anxious after the show when Avril wanted to venture outside to the back alley to say hello to some fans, as sometimes fans let their emotions get the better of them and can do unintended harm to their hero. I kept a close presence with her, but all went well. This was **Avril's My-Dad's-Neck-Tie** phase, but one thing you should never do is wear something like a scarf or necktie out in public if you're a Rock or Pop Star, as it can be grabbed and you could have the living daylights choked out of you; it's risky business.

My wife Lynne was the BMG Vancouver Office Coordinator for Avril's Sales and also ensured the early success of the record, being appointed Western Canada Sales Coordinator.

LED ZEPPELIN-

Never worked with them, but when I was with TPC/Quality, we did have their first LP, and when we put it on our woefully inadequate stereo, it scared the pants off us.

What fresh Hell is THIS?!

We'd never heard anything like it before, and we thought it was *LOUD*, which is funny now. It was a highly amplified, electric version of American Blues; no **Willie Dixon**, no **Led Zeppelin.**

The previous summer at the PNE, a group called **The New Yardbirds** played the Gardens Auditorium (Cap: 3000), fulfilling contractual dates, and left the audience totally stunned and stoned; meet **Led Zeppelin.**

They came back as **Zep** opening for **Iron Butterfly** (Pacific Coliseum), who returned the favor on their return date, and the rest is history. While I personally didn't meet them, my friend **Bruce Bissell** did, and HE'S got stories, best heard to the tune off "He Came In Thru the Broken Rear Limo Window" or something.

I think they were also the backing band on **Donavan's "Hurdy Gurdy Man"** as well.

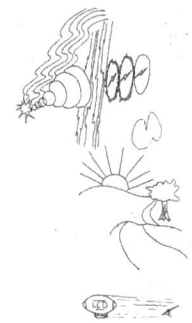

This serves to illustrate the two polar opposites of Led Zeppelin's Power side of their shredding the sound barrier and their ambient, bucolic, Celtic acoustic side. Also, a colouring book for the addled

CARLTON LEE-

He worked for **Tom Lavin's Powder Blues Band** and **Blue Wave Studios**.

Oddly, I was instrumental in getting him hired thru a request from my starter wife's work. He was a Chinese gent from Jamaica. He did some engineering on the Stones' ***Goats Head Soup*** LP and brought me up to speed on those guys. He lived in Richmond too, and we'd hook up after work for beers and shoot the breeze. Tom and I still get along, but diabetes got the best of Carlton. A good man and I miss him.

LYING-

Record Promo guys (in particular) were considered by the Great Unwashed Public to be a life form somewhere between a Used Car Salesman and a Carny Side-Show Shill.

Most of the ones I've known weren't, that's an American concept, and I personally resent it.

I have seen people who tried the tact of using great panic-stricken fables designed to invoke sympathy for their project and move that ahead, BUT, that has a downside: it doesn't work. What WILL happen if you're caught out in a lie or "enhancement" is your cred will be destroyed, and you'll be done.

While I never lied, I did…um…flesh out the truth, yeah. Sometimes, when pitching a record, I'd make up terms like "Texture Record," and when they inevitably said "Huh?" I'd qualify by saying how it fit in with the Musical Landscape of the Radio Station.

The actual correct term would be "Segue," but if I had their attention and leaning my way, why change dicks in the middle of a screw?

I save my bigger whoppers for home. I'm not very good at it as the use of my full name (**RAY-MOND**!) gets a lot of airtime when I'm found out, so much so our 2 & ½ year old Grandson has taken to calling me that instead of his "Gumpy" (Grumpy Grandpa).

I save most of my juicier lies for Special Occasions when I'll burn a song for my wife, usually something by **John Hiatt** cuz he just **NAILS** it, and then say that I wrote it for her!

THE LINCOLNS-

Every now & again, you come across a truly outstanding band; I've seen a few.

Tool was one, I didn't "get" the records, pretty dark and twisty stuff, but when I saw them live, the light went on. **The Dave Matthews Band** was another one, brilliant actually, altho the first time I saw them at an **RCA** Convention in **Seattle**, they went right over my head…ZOOM! However, when I saw them again at Vancouver's bastion of Counter-Culture, the **Town Pump**..BAM! It clicked, and at that point, I swore they were the **BEST** band I had ever seen.

And then…there was **The Lincolns**, a Toronto R&B outfit we happened to see at the end of a day during another **RCA** Sales meeting. This group was put together by Bassist extraordinaire **Prakash John** (who played on **Lou Reed's** incredible *Rock & Roll Animal* album), fronted by **Stephen**

Ambrose, the son of Canadian crooner **Tommy Ambrose**, and including several others, including Anne Murray's drummer the night I saw them; simply awesome.

That night, all the Promo guys were herded over to the club where, after becoming "like minded" we entered a standard darkened room. The band was tuning up, and the singer looking like a Maitre'D from a '50's snooty eatery: pink jacket, bow tie and slicked back hair. He smiled and gave us a "float wave"; what the Hell is THIS? I thought, and then the band KICKED in, he opened his mouth to sing and they tuned **US** up. We all sat there Gobsmacked by what we heard; it was amazing. The next day I recall gushing to **RCA Pres Ed Preston** about them and wanting him to sign them. They didn't.

The Lincolns did get a record out but I don't recall it flying on the airwaves, their live dynamic didn't translate to vinyl. Usually, bands don't do 'Live' recordings until later in their career, but in this case, it may have put them across sooner than later, but, that night, in that club, they were **AMAZING** to behold.

DEE LIPPINGWELL-

Rocktographer to the Stars! "No Flash" in the pan, she! If you don't see Dee smiling, the end is near.

Check out her latest book, "*First Three Songs, NO Flash*".

www.deelippingwell.com

CHATTER #10

LOVERBOY-

Thought this band was great! Played "**Working for the Weekend**" every Friday on the drive home with the volume up til the windshield almost crystallized. Had one record later on **CMC** (we called it the *C*lub for *M*idlife *C*rises), but not a single station in their home town would touch it, too bad. I worked hard for them and they were appreciative and respectful.

LYNNE-(LOVERGIRL)

THANKS to my wife for living thru all this and THAT, which has to be as difficult as *I* can be. I'm going to clone her in case she starts to wear out; besides, I don't know where she put everything! Yep, I chased her til she caught me.

An example of how interesting life with Lynne can be: She used to dye/streak her hair different spots and splashes of colour, something like a broken prism, and I learned when she did that, she'd just bought something. One day I came home all beat, and she hands me a small jeweler's box and tells me to open it (cuz I'm stupid?), and I do, and it's a key; "it's a key," I said, master of understatement that I am, "What for?" She replied, all excited…"I bought a Deli!"

"Par'Me?"

"I bought the Deli in **Steveston**, I LOVE their soup!"

"Par'Me?"

I was so stunned I couldn't even hear Jesus weeping behind me. So, that's how we started **Lynne's' Deli**, a true family operation.

Another time, the same key trick; "OK, so these are for Chrysler and you already have a Plymouth Voyager, I don't get it," I said, preparing for the worst.

"I bought a PT Cruiser!" she said with great delight.

Par'Me?

It's soup, I thought, it's the soup again..."So, is it souped up or something?" "No, she said, I just love it and its right outside!" So I work up the nerve to have a peek and there it is, our brand-new Silver Automatic Monthly withdrawal.

It's been a very interesting 33 years (as of this writing)...Surprise!!

There's lots more on this subject but I'll save that for another time, including doing a rewrite on the **"Honeymoon in Hell"** story so I'll be seen in a better light.

My lovely, LONG-suffering wife & meself at a Junos after-party

LYNYRD SKYNYRD-

We had (what was left of) them at **BMG** on the **CMC** label (recycled former glory) and a tour date to support the album.

I caught a call from a writer (name not mentioned) all agog about the new record and concert date, wanting a phone interview, so I put the request thru the system and got it done in good order.

The interview came out the day before the show and it was most, if not all of, an entire page, glorious!...except for one small detail... read it over 3 times and couldn't find any mention of the new record, which is how we make money; the Concert Promoter makes the money from the show.

In the Print Biz, there's a Rule of Thumb: unless you are a **BIG** act, if you get advance press, it's unlikely there'll be a concert review, and while Lynyrd Skynyrd were legendary, they were only a "Big" act.

So, in a colossal act of restraint, I called the writer and thanked him for the coverage, but asked where any mention of the new record was. Their response was...oh, I guess I forgot...to which I replied...so, can you tell me what OTHER **F**king** reason they're out on tour for? They said they'd TRY for a CD review, but as much as I've done to ward off Glaucoma, I don't recall ever seeing one for the concert or record; some people require a short leash.

THE MACARENA (WE CALLED IT THE HAIRBALL SONG)...

Yep, my fault, here anyways. There were competing versions, but mine won?

LARRY MACRAE-

A GREAT guy and friend from BMG. He was National Promotions; I called him Lawrence-of-a-Radio.

My old Boss Lawrence-of-a-Radio, overjoyed he's finally getting rid of me and able to remove the Steel reinforcing bars from his In-Box. Shooter–Dee Lippingwell

RAY MCAULEY & WILD COUNTRY-

Good guys, Great talent, and then Ray died, April 13 1978.

A local Surrey group, they had one LP ...***Sometimes Good, Sometimes Bad***... which sold fairly well for us at **RCA,** but then Ray died of a brain aneurism suddenly with not much left in the vaults. Two years later after getting feedback that the public was hungry, locally anyway, for more of Ray, we decided to do a posthumous 2nd LP ***Memories***, which Guitar Star and a man with a way with words, **Ed Molyski** put together; Ed was the group's writer in residence

We launched it two years after Ray passed at the Rootin, Tootin **Newton Inn**. It was a busy day; **RCA Canada President Ed Preston** was in town to finish up signing the **Powder Blues Band**, and the launch was that night, a Monday. The show sold out to the rafters. I put the whole thing on basically single-handedly with benefits to the **BC Country Music Association** and featuring the CREAM of the area's talent; it was a night to remember. We had TV, Press, and Radio people, and **Ed Preston** giving **Ed Molyski** and **Elaine McAuley** the first framed **GOLD** copies of the LP on-stage, to everyone's delight.

Not to brag (he said bragging) but to sell out a 450-seat room on a rainy Monday night was rather special. Now Ray lives on in Legend, and we all miss him still.

When I took the single from the *Memories* LP to **Radio CKWX**, I was in high anticipation, but that turned to dread and anxiety shortly, as the Music Director, **Weird Harold** took his time listening to it in the library, not saying a word. Then, finally he turns to me and says, "I dunno, Ray's not breathing right"; my reply was "Jesus Christ, Harold, Ray's not breathing at all now, he's DEAD!" They did add the single, but good grief!

Ray and some young strumpet looking her breast.

CHATTER #11

MARTINA MCBRIDE-

My friend Bruce Allen's act. What a talent, and she might have broken bigger if my "**Runaway McBride**" Promo was allowed to happen...sigh, always a Runaway Bridesmaid.

I recall being away from the office and Bruce calling about some stock issues in the stores. Somebody that should have known better had the nerve to tell Bruce, the act's Manager, that "it was just a County Act!" Open mouth, change feet. I wondered where Bruce planned on hiding the body.

"**Where would you be**" is still one the **BEST** tracks ever done, especially the live version; passion doesn't come any better than that.

Martina's first Canadian GOLD!
Actually an appetizer; we ALL wanted Platinum
(L>R) Kim Blake (BATA), the wonderful Michelle Stewart-BMG BC Branch Manager, Heck Ramsay BMG Promo Nabob, Bruce being loose, and BMG BC's Miss Katherine, a true Professional and Friend. Photo Courtesy of Dee Lippingwell.

TERRY MCBRIDE-

The other part of Vancouver's Pop Power Triumvirate. Always on a Workaholiday. Astute and well respected. Deals with everything head on, no phone messages for THIS guy! Dealt with him on Avril day to day during that project and **Treble Charger** too.

CRAIG MCDOWELL, MCM CONCERTS-

Whether it was Rock, Rasslin' or Country, Craig did it all with style.

KRIS MCKAY: MY SUGARMAN-

In my careen thru the Record Industry, my greatest failure has been being unable to put **Kris McKay's** *What Love Endures* project where it rightfully belongs. To me, this is a rare gem, an absolutely fucking BRILLIANT body of work. Don't matter it came out in 1990, good and even GREAT music is timeless. This is my Sugarman, my Rodriguez.

It took some digging, but I turned up a video for the best track on the LP, the bombastic "**The Bigger the Love**" (if *THAT* doesn't move you, you have to be heartless)

... and here's ANOTHER treat, check out the video link to one of the **BEST** songs you may ever hear, from the album you've **NEVER** heard: "**If Ever You Need Me.**"

Reco: The Bigger the Love (SonicHits) If ever you need me

Kris McKay If ever you need me- (YouTube)

Play it forward...

Footnote: Recently I've heard **Howie Mandel** on some Music show on TV gush about one of the contestants and really build her up, which was nice, BUT he cited when **Clive Davis**, the Patron Saint of Discovering Rock music all by himself, went to the **Monterey Pop Fest** and "discovered" the band "that NOBODY had EVER heard of, **Big Brother & the Holding Company** with **Janis Joplin** on Vocals," and single-handedly made them stars, except for the fact that several people DID already KNOW about them, maybe half of California? You see, they already had an LP out on the boutique **Vanguard** label, which the company I worked for, **TPC/Quality**, had in the catalogue. Good for Clive, but **Kris McKay** is the Janis he missed.

CATHERINE MCKINNON-

Don Harron's (a VERY nice guy) wife, but THIS Banshee taught me to screen my off-hour calls at home when she called one Sunday night to say she was in town (Huh?!) and called Radio about her new single (just delivered), and she was FREAKING OUT cuz whoever she spoke to said they couldn't find it (it's right over *THERE*, meathead!). I had **NO** idea what **Quality Promo** told her that I could do, but I DO know what I told her *she* could do, and we haven't spoken since.

She was also Canada's equivalent of **Anita Bryant**, the Orange Juice talking head who gained instant fame for her remarks about Gay People. One good talking head deserves another I suppose.

MURRAY MCLAUCHLAN-

His "**La Guerre C'est Fini Pour Moi**" was probably one of the first songs I recognized as being Triple A (A3), altho at the time that Radio format did not exist.

I consider it something of a masterpiece, so there. Another album track of his that's a stand-out is his tribute to Circus Clown **Emmet Kelly**, the original sad-face clown, called "**Sweeping the Spotlight Away**," which was a part of Emmet's routine. I saw Murray perform this on TV and I've never forgotten it, and this was before the repetition of Video to remind me. Once, I saw it once. Going on about Emmet, if anyone's interested, there is a story about Emmet's single tear on his make-up which bears googling. It's heartwarming and touching and **Stephen King** even threw to that in his book *It*.

I haven't been able to locate a linkable video for the stunning (to me at least) performance of this song from the CBC TV special **"On the Boulevard"** 1976, but there is this "video" of the song; just not the performance of it.

Reco- Murray McLauchlan, "Sweeping the Spotlight Away," "La Guerre C'est Fini Pour Moi:

I never met Murray, but I do know and have worked with his wife **Denise Donlon** who came up thru the ranks from working **Doug & the Slugs** with **Feldman**, then soared to the lofty height of running **Sony Canada**.

MCMASTER & JAMES-

We had BMG Duo **McMaster & James** in town to escape their hometown of Winnipeg and to do Promo for their *Love Wins Every Time* CD; one promotion was a telephone interview to **Radio Z95** from their hotel room, and during that, they told everyone (read: everywoman) their hotel and room #, at which point I was calling the Jock on-air and was on him like a wet shirt to **STOP** announcing that! You NEVER let out where an Artist/Group is staying, God knows what can result. In this case, however, either I got to the station in time or we had a lot more work to do, as nothing went down, or up, for that matter.

I saw part of my job as developing the artist's profile thru the Media to the public so they could be recognized in restaurants, and later, afford to eat in them.

CHARLIE MAJOR-

SIX consecutive Number Ones from his debut *Lucky Man* CD, and a bitter man, after Radio changed their way of reporting, BUT a BETTER MAN today as he's re-releasing his first hit **"It Can't Happen To Me"** with a stampede of today's Country talent; what the hell, it worked for **Santana!**

Here's the 411 from FYI, Canada's Music Industry journal

https://www.fyimusicnews.ca

– On Aug. 17, Canadian country star **Charlie Major** releases the 25th anniversary edition of his #1 hit single "It Can't Happen To Me," via MDM Recordings Inc./UMC. This new version features an A-list grouping of peers, including Dean Brody, Terri Clark, Johnny Reid, Gord Bamford, Jess Moskaluke, Derek Miller, Jason Blaine, Tim Hicks, The Road Hammers, Doc Walker, Bobby Wills, Brett Kissel, Jason McCoy, Aaron Pritchett, Aaron Goodvin and Tebey. All proceeds go to MADD Canada. Major's next album, *More Of The Best (Greatest Hits 2)*, arrives Sept. 7. Major is currently playing western dates supporting Alabama.

www.charliemajor.com

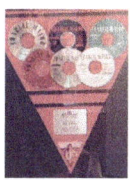

Charlies 6 consecutive #1s plaque issued to the Promo Reps that got it done!

BOB MARLEY-

A "highly" hypnotic performer. I recall meeting them at the airport, and the Promoter had **NO** manifest for customs, who were busy snapping on rubber gloves, nor transport for what appeared to be some kind of colorful Caribbean street festival taking place in front of us all. Meanwhile, their Tour Manager, with a holster of Hash Pipes on his belt, was trying to sort this all out. I was pretty sure the group could have saved a LOT of money by not using a plane to fly in, they were doing fine on their own. And thanks to Bob as well for clarifying that "Ganja" is dope and not an affectionate term for an older relative.

SHOOTING MARLEY-

The one time I worked with Ras **Bob Marley & the Wailers** in Vancouver, there was a backstage incident worth noting. Sometime prior to his concert date here at the **QET**, Bob survived being shot, with a handgun (by Johnny Too Bad?), and I had charge of an overeager fan with a camera wanting to take his picture, but I couldn't allow it. Incensed, she **DEMANDED** to know why, and I explained it was because she had a regular "Flash" and not a "Black Flash" (which the Pros use). She then wanted to know what the difference was, and I explained that there's little difference between a regular camera "Flash" and a gun muzzle "flash" (except for the sound), and considering he had just recovered from being ventilated, I'm sure he'd feel safer and give a better performance having not had to endure the picture, so, **NO**.

So, the guy survives being shot but succumbs to a "pimple" on his toe, which turned out to be Cancer, there's no Jah-stice.

Reco- Bob Marley, "One Love" (MUSIC VIDEO)

MAROON 5-

They came to us, like the **Dave Matthews Band**, with a year-old album, but hard work gave us similar results, only sooner! They played here so often I was beginning to think they were local. Their album was a hit, then they buggered off.

Reco- Maroon 5, "Wakeup Call"

MATTHEW GOOD/BAND

A rather extraordinary Good story, as he morphed from a solo Folkist into a full blown Rocker basically in his own hook, and the band fast became a Fox (Radio) "house band" joining the ranks of **Heart, BTO, Chilliwack, Loverboy, Headpins, Nickelback** (who were available to us at **RCA**, but **Warner's** had the foresight to strike first), **Treble Charger**, and the revered **T Hip**, among others.

I didn't get to work with him directly (**Mercury** having *their* eye on the ball in this case), altho we passed thru the hallowed halls of **The Fox**, but we were in an orbit of a kind, as he was a fan of our band **Copyright** and went so far as to say during an interview on the Fox that Copyright was a better band than his own! Heady stuff!

Next, Matthew is headlining a concert in Victoria at the old Memorial Arena along with another of ours, **Treble Charger**.

As this was to be a busy gig, I took the indomitable **Mike Moreau**, my assistant, with me so we could split up the work.

That afternoon we did all our Media work with the bands, and everything went swimmingly until we arrived at the arena and the undertow took hold; we found that all the previously approved backstage passes/accreditations had been cut back, including my own!

Somehow Mike was OK, but I seriously needed to be back there. A storm of cell phone calls ensued, only to find that the Promoter only had **ONE** cell for his crew, and it didn't work in all the areas (Jesus H Jumpin' Christ, what *IS* this, Rock & Roll?!). Then, finally I got thru to the Production Manager, and the door opened JUST in time for us to see the power go out midway thru **Copyright's** set…is this gig cursed?!

Power restored, they finished their bit, altho noisus interruptus, and next up was **Treble Charger**, who were unhappy their rider was reduced…is there no END to this?

So, that's the Close Encounter version. Having said that, I've always LOVED two tracks from Matthew's "***Underdogs***" album, "***Prime Time Deliverance***," and "***Change of Season***," neither of which were big radio hits I don't think, but that notwithstanding, I find them both to be exquisitely BRILLIANT, and the very epitome of what Modern Rock, and ROCK itself to be. So please treat yourself if you haven't yet, here's the links and I hope this is Good for you too!

Reco- Matthew Good Band, "Prime Time Deliverance," "Change of Season"

CHATTER #12

(I hear you Rappin', but you can't come in!)

MetaForest-A Post Raytirement project.

Word….

For the most part I think that people that make Rap Music should be shot with their own weapons. There **ARE** some nice people in it, and some good music too, just not a lot. **Kris Parker from KRS1** was a gentleman; I was expecting to be killed. Before I went to meet him I was listening to his new LP and tripped on the line, "Let's smash a bottle in his face and kill whitey!" Hang on..*I'M* whitey!

Swollen Members did well, but most white people can't Rap. I know I can't; I tried but I just spit on myself. And those hand gestures? I'm not "signing," man, that's Arthritis!

Eminem did some good stuff, but the first record of his I heard had **SO** much language in it and was so heavily beeped on the Radio, it sounded like a busy signal on a phone line. Kids **LIKE** bad language. I remember talking to **Odds** about putting a Parental Awareness sticker on *their* record; there were no language issues, but kids would have bought it BECAUSE it *said* there was.

So *anyways*, the **Metaforest** project actually came to my house, escorted by a couple of members of a Motorcycle Admirers club, definitely NOT Heaven sent (cough), and I turned it down, but not without repetition;

these guys are like a hungry German Shepherd eating treats, they don't understand the term "all done"

A year later, he's back, on his own, and I agreed to work it **provided** he wasn't remotely associated with as much as an in-line skate club! It was still a LOT of work. I got him Management, **Frank Weipert**, but he STILL came to me when he got stopped by American Customs at YVR and was refused entry to the U.S. for a previous, um...Peccadillo concerning a controlled substance. He complained it was unfair, but I reminded him "you know you have a freakin' SNAKE tattoo on your neck, right? People that look like YOU scare people like THEM." I pointed him towards an Immigration Lawyer, but he did an end run and **WALKED** across the border at Abbotsford the next day! This would be what? Homeland Insecurity?

When he got back from the States, he wanted me to come see him perform at a Rap club but I refused, citing, "I'm in bed hours if not DAYS before you even *think* about going on stage, AND there's a hospital right down the street so I can stay home and shoot myself and save the time, travel and inconvenience of going to get shot in Vancouver." He didn't disagree.

*A Rapper's Alphabet~ um...a, b. c, *d*, THC...uh...

CHATTER #13

MIDNITE RODEO BAND-

A result of my association with **Ed Molyski** from **Ray McAuley & Wild Country**; signed them to **RCA**. **Jess Lee** is a Classic Country singer, possibly the BEST Honky-Tonk singer in Canada. Good Experience, Ed in an expensive studio trying to find that Special/Magic lick that only Bats and Hamsters can hear. Ed, along with **Treachers Records** owner and good friend **Richard Watt**, helped bring them and **Bonnie James** to National Prominence. They were nominated and won Regional Country Awards (BC Country Music Association) and also received multiple nominations for National Awards (Canadian Country Music Association), including the **Juno Awards**. They were ahead of their time.

MRB & Me
(L>R) Big Al (looming over...), Chris,
Ed, Heck Ramsay (2nd Fiddle), Jess (holding up his pants)
Shooter-Bennett Wong

Reco Rodeo…

MRB-Nashville just wrote another cheatin' song link www.youtube.com/watch?v=LOZqP61Gw5Y

MRB Reunion Link www.youtube.com/watch?v=RTOSBZMWp3A

All tracks written by Ed Molyski, Vocals-Jess Lee

ED MOLYSKI (AGAIN)-

Personifies Country Music.

Two groups he was in achieved a high degree of success, notably Ray McAuley & Wild Country and Midnite Rodeo Band (MRB), where he was songwriter, guitarist and clothes horse.

Ed is a 6-string savant. He virtually builds his own guitars and sound effects.

He started playing part time while working at Cummins Diesel, but wanted to play so bad he took a gig (and a train) to **Churchill, Manitoba** (to play for Inuit and hungry Polar bears?), and never looked back or got up early again.

He has a deep affinity for **Don Rich**, guitar innovator from **Buck Owens** & the **Buckaroos** that helped shape the **"Bakersfield Sound,"** a genre whose biggest successes were **Buck** and **Merle Haggard**. This is surprising, since **Nashville** covets its own like a spoiled child. People who don't 'cut' in Nashville don't get much support (read: Full Ignore), ask **Dwight Yoakam** or **Sara Evans** who both "cut" in **California**. The irony in Sara's case is the title of her first, very quietly received, LP was *Three Chords & the Truth*, which is a quote from Country Master Songwriter **Harlan Howard** when he was asked what makes a good Country song; her 2nd LP 'cut' in Nashville, was HUGE, Huh.

At one **BC Country Music Awards** show, **Jess Lee (MRB)** had won the **Male Vocalist** award, and when accepting his honor, tipped his hat to Ed, saying, "A lot of people think Ed Molyski can't sing, but he taught ME how to sing with Soul, so that's Bull!" High praise indeed.

Ed also has a massive Pig collection: Plastic Pigs, Plush Pigs, frozen Bacon, Ceramic Pigs; a collection of Snouters that would rival anything Jimmy Dean could scare up on the hoof!

BONNIE JAMES-

An INTENSE & PASSIONATE *Dynamo* of a singer, songwriter and performer. She walked up to the Breakout line but wouldn't cross it. What a Talent, gone too soon but not forgotten.

Bonnie Rippin' it up at the 1981 Molson Danny Awards
Now known at the BC Country Music Awards

ANNE-MARIE DE LA GERODAY-

A Post Raytirement project from my friend from Bars we both worked (and drank) at. She's an Actress, Performer and Singer too. And in my opinion, she's got **it**. She's certainly got the eyes for "it." Not everyone gets that at this point, but she does and they will.

I'm just trying to help, NOT get into Management, having raised my own kids. One day, soon I hope, some Entertainment Nabob will hear what I see. Go to YouTube and peep "To Make You Feel my love", "I'll be seeing you", and certainly "New Year's Eve".

Here is Anne Marie singing "Waitress (the Dream)" written by R's truly, Down Home Jerome and Anne!

Anne-Marie, "The Waitress," Country ROCK: https://youtu.be/drTJbozxo10

Anne-Marie, "The Waitress," Country: https://youtu.be/2DqYk_iUlk

MOBY-

What a **GREAT** and enjoyable project, and an equally great guy.

Persistence is **PLATINUM** and we **PROVED** that.

Ain't no Moby 'bout it!
Here's the man himself backstage at 'Richards' with the BMG Van Crew. (L>R) Me, Mr Funky-Pants holding a copy of **Play** *one of the BEST albums ever, Dale Robertson-BMG Van, that* **Moby** *guy (Center), Our Mel-BMG Van, Miss Katherine-BMG Van, (Front Row) the Lovely Lisa-BMG Van, Street Rep Guy-Dean Pogue BMG Van.*
Photo courtesy of some guy with a camera.

MONTY PYTHON'S FLYING CIRCUS-

My **BIG** coming out promo, and a career-defining campaign; we **SET** records, we **SOLD** records, we laughed, we cried, what a bunch of LOONS!

Ticket sales for their run of shows in Vancouver were inexplicably slow. We had them on the **Charisma** label, their **first** LP being '*Another Monty Python Record*', and the **second** being *The Previous Monty Python Record*. The first LP was a cover of a Classical LP with black pen crossing out the original name and scrawling in the Python stuff. On the back was the Liner Notes, which started off reviewing a Classical record before merging into coverage of a tennis match, leave it to them.

To help raise awareness for the records and the shows, I came up with the idea of building a cage on the back of a Flat-Bed truck, complete with signage, and having that drive around Vancouver's main roads, especially in rush hour.

The day the group arrived, I had the truck go to the airport with clearances from DOT, and was awaiting them in the lot. I had also hired a RED London-style double-decker bus to transport all of us to the hotel adorned with Union Jacks and concert signage, if memory serves; this made the heady speed of 10 MPH.

The group arrived in something of a besotted condition (they were pissed) and, armed with squirt-guns, were soaking each other and some international flight people with what we all prayed was water and not *previously enjoyed* water, the 'p' being the clue here. They had just spent the day at Banff at a book signing for their new tome "**Monty Python's Big Red Book**," which was, of course, **Blue**…those guys!

Leaving the terminal, we were greeted by fans who had been tipped by the Press (LOVE those guys!); the group got into the cage for publicity photos, and once that was done, utterly destroyed the cage within about 2 minutes. No mess, however; the fans took the wreckage home for souvenirs!

We went onto the bus and crawled into town; I recall while we were reviewing our planned Promo activities, **Dr. Graham Chapman** kept asking where the 'Poufter'(sic) clubs were, but not being on that team, we really didn't know, and in those days, nothing was open on Sundays. The next few days were JAMMED with Media activities, and the Promoter **Hugh Pickett** advised me that all this resulted in setting a Box Office record for ticket sales!

I thoroughly enjoyed working with them all, oddly the most serious, if not least sane, was **John Cleese**, but Comedy IS a serious business.

Here's R's truly ready for my cage match with Monty Python's Flying Circus. The 2nd pic is them caged and me ready to split before they DESTROYED the cage mere seconds later, the bastards! #41-Pythons enraged encaged w Ray in the back This is June 1973, Photo / L Courtesy of John Mahler. R/ Courtesy Gary Cullen

Just another Ray in the Life.

This is one of the funniest videos I think I've seen from **ANYONE..**

I can't link to it but Highly **reco** this clip: **Monty Python, "Fish Dance"**

CHATTER #14

Musician, Heal Thyself-(OK, THAT'S a stretch, but 'Music Man' didn't work)

Following my surgery for Cancer I continued to work, even in the Hospital, just to show you what a Pressure-Hound I can be.

I have to go for a Colonoscopy every 5 years. If you don't know what that procedure is, plainly speaking, they fill you full of REALLY good dope and THEN send a Camera Crew up your butt...*Bump* Hey, really low ceiling in here!

The 1st time I endured this, after languishing in a hallway while I got so high I could go Duck hunting with a rake while playing some tunes on the Butt-Trumpet to amuse myself, I finally got wheeled into a room where the procedure begins..**OW**! Pardon Me! Have we met?! Then, the Dr. asks if I'd like to watch this on the monitor (What, no movies?), and I beg off, telling him that too many people think I have my head up my ass as it is and I don't want to give that notion any credibility.

Then, as I'm zoning away, watching Plastercine Porters wearing Marshmallow Ties, he interjects and says he has a class of Medical Students observing (**WHAT!?**), and do I mind? **Hell Yeah!** Came to mind, but I was powerless to stop it, and there they are, all smiling and waving (God I hate my life).

Now, I've had a few, ummmm, intrusions (from those Butt-Inskies), but the last one was different, as I'd never been interviewed before the procedure. A very nice lady, looked like a Haus Frau volunteer, started asking me several mundane questions, like name, age, do I know where "up" is, and things like that. THEN she asks if I've ever used Marijuana, Hashish, Cocaine, LSD…and at that point I broke into her litany and said "Lady? I'm in the Music Business, what do YOU think?" At that point she got very small and quiet and walked away. And THAT'S how this story ties into the Biz; the Music/Proctology Mix.

CHATTER #15

VAN MORRISON-

Never met him, but I did meet one of his band members, who told me to never to get in a vehicle with him if he was driving because he was the world's worst driver, probably invented "Off Road" driving single handedly.

My opinion of Van is this: God invented Music and then created Van Morrison to sing it for him.

Reco- "Cleaning Windows" is an undiscovered working man's anthem if ever there was.

MÖTLEY CRÜE/AUTOGRAPH-

This was the night before the **Thompson Twins** concert, and as contrasted as much as Day from Night. We had the opening act **Autograph**, which had a new LP out, and hit single, their Paean to the Gods of the Airwaves, "**Turn Up the Radio**!" While they were trying to tear a hole in the Sound Barrier with that opus, I wandered around the Coliseum taking note of the fans in their rather Goth "Angel of Death" clothing look, huffing on hemp and having casual sex in doorways and nooks (nookies?) along the Concourse (Uh…it says *CON*-course NOT *INTER*-course!), and I wound up backstage in the **Mötley Crüe** area. That was the first time I met them; we had a couple of their later albums and things ran hot and cold, but nothing bad, but then I wasn't **Steve Newton.**

So here I am with them, all the hair and make-up and **BLACK** and glitter, very pleasant, and then I saw the bevy of young nubiles, all dressed for human sacrifice, and you KNOW didn't look like that when they left their parents' houses and I left at that point, before one of their armed and angry fathers showed up. What a circus.

I think this was around **MC's "Smokin' in the Boys Room"** days. I remember the single, as it was a cover of the **Brownsville Station** hit I had promoted. I remember that band because of the drummer, whose name was Henry "H-Bomb" Weck. He was as *loud* as one.

MR. MISTER-

Mr. Mister was a big deal with their first LP, and girls just LOVED **Richard Page**, the lead guitarist/Vocalist. We were in **Kelowna** for a show, and the group had done their Meet & Greet Fan/Retail/Media due diligence and retired to their dressing room when a rather disorganized Time Sales Rep from the "Presenting" Station came up to me and demanded I bring them out to meet some of his Spur-of-the-moment newfound friends. I had to tell him no, they were done for the night. He then attempted to barge into their dressing room, and I stopped him, telling him that wasn't happening either. Then he rained curses down on me and said I was a Big Shot, Big City Asshole, taking over in "his" town; correct.

So this is going on and it's chaos backstage where they took all the fainting & injured concert goers that had dropped like flies during the show, and this Jack-Ass wouldn't let up, so I ended by telling him that I'd been doing this for a while and have known his boss so long that I know his real name and will be having a word with him about you, **Ass Hole**. I heard no more about it after my talk with his boss, so maybe he's gone from selling Time to doing it.

TERRY DAVID MULLIGAN, AKA TDM-

A lot has been said of him, some of it by me, but at the end of the day he got the job done. Perennially effervescing about Music and Canadian music in particular. I donated pics for the Mulligan Stew opus. I'll always thank him for getting me to **"The Alamo,"** it's a shirt-off-the back thing

CHATTER #16

A TOAST TO TED!

This is a sidebar about breaking records on the Radio, and involves a totally unknown artist, **Hansie**, from Holland on the **Millennium** label. As it crossed my desk one day, I popped it on, and what I heard was so hot it almost burst into flames on my turntable (google it), so the first thing I did was call **Ted Wendland** (then **Music Director at CFMI-FM** now better known as **Rock 101**), who was always open to hot new tracks. I told him I had a combustible tune and was on my way out (to their then studios in **New Westminster**, now the **TD/Black Tower** in downtown Vancouver), when I got there, he played it once and immediately agreed this HAD to be HEARD. So, satisfied, I drove back to my office only to hear him play it as I drove away! I bet **THAT** doesn't happen anymore.

As my business was about growing the awareness of the hit, I sent it to CJIB in Vernon. They played it, and their phones lit up. I took THAT and Ted's support to Don Stevens at then-Top 40 Powerhouse CKLG, who was impressed enough to add it to their station. That triggered their sister station CHED in Edmonton, but little else seemed to follow nationally, no idea why.

Keep in mind this was 1979 and you could still do that fun stuff back then.

Reco- Put your seatbelt on and take a spin with Hansie on YT

MIKE NESS-

Good God, WHAT a talent. Another tortured soul with mega talent, nobody should make a Country record before they hear his.

Reco- Mike Ness, "Ballad of a Lonely Man"

CHATTER #17

THE NEWTON INN-

Has a new owner now, Jimmy Pattison, and it's been renamed **SaveOn Foods**; yep! The only Country things there now are the Hams in the Meat Department.

But...once it was the Rootin, Tootin, **Newton**, the lower mainlands HOME of **Country Music**; the first time I had an act play there I had to phone them for directions how to get there, and this is what the receptionist told me.."Y'know sweetie, Surrey is the Asshole of BC and Newton is 5 miles up it" (True!)

Back then it was run by **Ron Abrams,** and very successfully. One of the reasons was he picked up a LOT of "routing" tour dates from American artists near the border looking to fill a date and an easy payday.

Possibly my most outstanding (I won't say fondest) memory of the Newton Inn was one morning after working with an act that played the night before, I went down to their restaurant for breaky and ordered Sausages & Eggs. imagine my surprise when I was served Eggs and **WEINERS!!** Well, this was a whole new **bawl** game, and I demanded from the waitress tell me just what this was, and she told me they were all out of sausages, and what's the problem, the wieners were the same shape! And she was dead serious! Hmm, sounds like there's a 12-inch Pianist joke sneaking in here.

NSYNC/BOY OH BOY BANDS-

I refuse to call groups like these Boy BANDS, as bands, to me, play instruments. They are a vocal group, meat puppets, and to try and dispel that idea they *were* that, at one show, the **Backstreet Boys** all put on instruments in an effort to spotlight their musicianship, kinda hard when there's a full band behind you playing over you, if you're even plugged in. But the girls went crazy and boy did they scream. I get the same result when I strap a guitar on, but they don't scream **PLAY!** They scream **RAY!** Put that goddam thing down and walk away! Yeah.

NSYNC backstage at The Forum during their 1st Vancouver date w R2 (1st on Left looking like their grandfather...sigh) and Miss Katherine (2nd from right) BMG Van, and the lovely Lisa BMG Van (right) and the indomitable Mike Moreau BMG Van kneeling, front row on right.

Still talking Boy Groups (Ha!), we had **NSYNC** in Van for show supporting their debut LP, and part of their Promo activities was an in-store Autograph signing at HMV Robson Street. It went swimmingly, drawing a very large crowd and selling a tsunami of product, but there was a flaw in the ointment: earlier in the day, as I was driving their Tour Manager somewhere, he informed me that the Private Soundcheck Party for Z95 contest winners, which had already run with their Management's approval, wasn't going to happen, as the group "didn't do those things," and I turned to him and stated, with a modicum of assurance and authority, that

"***TODAY** they're* **FUCKING DOING THAT!**" **a**nd they did! Otherwise, if Integrity had wings, it would have flown South that instant. However, everything worked out for everyone and all was good…

…until the next morning. When I got to my office, I caught a call from an obviously inebriated woman that was railing at me because she let her daughter go to downtown Vancouver (with another young friend) unsupervised to the **NSYNC** Autograph signing where said jeune fille was approached by a man telling her, for $5, he would give her the name of the hotel and room # where the band was staying, and she bought it, only to find there was no such hotel. She was out $5, but had come to no harm otherwise thank goodness.

Meanwhile, Mother-Of-The-Year slurred on and on about how this was all our **(BMG's)** fault, and I, realizing how pointless this all was, hung up on her after telling her that in no way were we responsible for her child. Then she told me she was an actress and I agreed with her; She probably played drunks.

About an hour later, I received another call from a very nice young lady, the aforesaid daughter, asking if her mother had called me. I said she had and how unhappy she was, and the girl, almost in tears, apologized profusely for that. I got her home addy and sent her some NSYNC Posters and swag, but stopped short of telling her that if that woman was MY mother, I'd sue her.

Shit happens, but why on Earth would you put your child in harm's way?

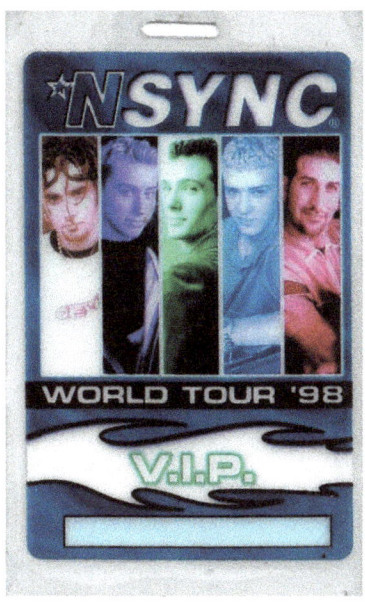

NEW YORK DOLLS-

This tarted-up bunch of misfits from the New Yawk/CBGB's scene blew right off the pages of **"Creem"** & **"Circus"** magazines and into a venue near you!

I was fascinated & got their debut LP right away; it was raw & exciting. The track I remember most, **"Trash,"** epitomized it.

As they were on another label, I did not get to work with them, but years later, I did meet & work with who may have been the only remaining living Doll, **David Johansen**. He was on **RCA** at the time under the persona of **Buster Poindexter**.

It's a good thing the press liked the record Bcuz Radio *RAN* from it. He did do a cookin' version of **"Hot, Hot, Hot!,"** a signature song of our **Parachute Club** as well.

I met him at one of our conventions in '88, and he was very amiable (at that time he had appeared as the Taxi driver in Bill Murray's *Scrooged* and he told me he was such a mess the morning he went to read for the part, he put Prep H under his eyes to make the bags look less puffy! I laughed like Hell!

There have been other incarnations of the NY Dolls, but the original worked the best.

David Johansen (aka Buster Poindexter) asking me if I can see any Prep H under his eyes.

ODDS-

My FAVORITE band. Cannot say enough about these guys, proud to know them all. I felt they were as close as I would get to working with **The Beatles**.

I BUSTED my shoes for these guys and I did deliver. Then they left the "**Zoo**" (their label) for Weiner Music, and I was told by their Promo rep **Chris Kennedy** that their debut single for them was the easiest record they ever took to radio; it walked in the door and right onto the air. You're welcome.

I recall **Drew Burns** from **The Commodore** calling me one day kvetching that he took a booking for **Odds**, and saying why should he pay them when they played down the street for free?! Well, yes/no; they had been the house band **"Dawn Patrol"** playing covers at the **Roxy** UNTIL they recorded and became **Odds**, and I WOULD show him why he should have taken the booking!

I developed an **INTENSE** Media campaign that saw me beat EVERY bush and overturn EVERY stone, which bore out a *great* reward when I climbed The Commodore's stairs and saw, at the top, a sign that read "SRO"! It was a high point of my career. Point made, point taken.

Altho I wasn't their Manager, when I heard that **Bryan Adams** was set to play **GM Place** (Now **Rogers Arena**), I called Bruce (until I thought he was going to charge me rent for living on his phone line) to try and get **Odds** on the show. Word was out that **Sass Jordan** was on the short list to open, and her vocal style was *somewhat* like Bryan's, a husky, throaty edge that works so well for Bryan, but I thought two of those was two too many, this was a Rock show, not a hoarse show.

It turned out that Bryan opted for the "An Evening With..." format, which was a great show in itself, and we didn't lose out to anyone, but not for lack of trying.

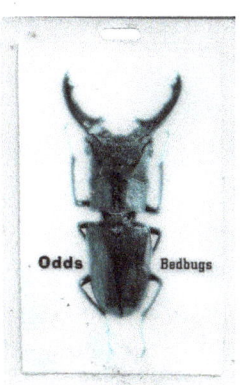

How much do I think of them? I recall, sometime after I stepped off the **BMG** stage, that I was listening to **100.3 The Q** (www.theq.fm) and heard **Scott James** muse on-air that they would be playing **Victoria** shortly, and he hoped to get an interview to advance that, so without thinking, I called **Craig Northey** and gave him all the contact 411 to get the interview done and **BAM!** It got done. It was simply 2nd nature for me to do that for them both, the Radio Station and the band.

When I went to **Dee Lippingwell's** *First Three Songs* Book release soiree, I got into my Rock stuff and had a choice between two T-Shirts: **The Beatles** and **Odds**. I chose **Odds** as it was an even chance **Sir Paul** wouldn't be there anyway, and I wanted to support my guys.

"Odds' Doug and Craig reuniting to play for my "Let's throw Raymond from the Gravy Train" send off @ The Roxy. What SUPER Guys to do that for me. Shooter-Dee Lippingwell

Reco- Odds, "Love is the Subject," "King of the Heap," "Heterosexual Man"

THE ORIGINAL SWING KIDS-

Sarah Vaughan, Count Basie, Mills Brothers, Joe Pass, Milt Jackson, Oscar Peterson; Smooth, Slick Professionals onstage and off, every one, what a pleasure to have had the opportunity.

BETH ORTON-

We REALLY tried for her; equal parts talent and torture, she could have been bigger.

CHATTER #18

OWLS-

A lot of people think the Music Biz is/was a piece of cake; listening to tunes, hanging with the stars, huffing Ganja, gorging and boozing on the company's dime, riding round in limos, going to bed late, rising later.

I don't know anybody that lived like that and, well…lived.

My day would start around 5:30 or 6AM and usually ran about 10 to 12 hours, sometimes up to 16/18, and once or twice I clocked in at 21 hours.

BUT no matter how long you work, you are STILL getting up early and you can't escape your job; if you turn on a Radio or TV, open a Newspaper, and now Social Media, you're working, it's all part of what you do.

When I hear younger people today whine about a HARD 8 hours, missing a Birthday or other Special Occasion, a weekend Long or otherwise, I think, TOUGH, my heart pumps Pee for you sniveler, wah-wah-wah.

There WERE perks and privilege but you *worked* for and *earned* them. We all get one (final) limo ride, but we'll be lying down for that.

Almost always a long day included an Artist/Band in concert, which started with making sure the Media/Retail itinerary was locked down and timed, then working the act thru the day, and, if they were playing a Club, a looooooong break between that and them actually playing, sometimes, the NEXT DAY.

A lot of people think Clubs are all about Music; they aren't. They're about selling booze and LOTS of it. The music is the means, which is why they play so late; they're kept off stage until the last possible moment, which could mean 1AM the day after they're advertised playing there. In **New York,** some clubs wouldn't start a band until 3 or 4 AM!

Club owners know that patrons sometimes get "high" before a show, and that's not new, but often people who smoke before a show don't drink as much as people that don't, and considering alcohol is a depressant, those people are "low." Club owners deal with that, but they really prefer that if you want a "Bud," you have one in a bottle or can instead of tightly wound rolling papers, ok?

Some Record Reps I knew could cat-nap in the lull before the **Sturm und Drang** and awake refreshed, but that never worked for me; I'd awake feeling like I'd been thrown into a Hay Baler, so I'd "go long" and endure. I believe I once wrote an instructive piece called "**What to do until the Band goes away**"; I'll have to dig that out.

One of my Longest Day groups was **The Cruzados,** a TexMex band from LA who were short on the Tex part, heavy on the Mex. I recall their guitarist **Marshal Rhoner** (now there's a good espanish name for you) had dyed his hair Black to fit in with the real Hombres, and when he took his wide-brimmed hat off, there was a very distinct and noticeable colour line between dirty blonde and pitch black; been on tour a while, Marshall?

So here I go to the **Town Pump,** home of the Night Owls and Early Birds, to see my band in action, and they wrap it all up with that chestnut "**La Bamba**" (SURPRISE!); it was hilarious to see the crowd singing along, murdering the lyrics in possibly Spanglish or maybe Pig-Latin.

The next day I wrote up this little gambit up for Head Office; I was so tired my hair hurt, and I asked if our bands were going to go on so late, could I buy **"Promo Owls"** and send THEM to see the groups, I mean, they're up all night anyway, right?

That idea didn't fly, but did limp its way to the overcrowded **"Ray's Bright Idea Orphanage"** where a LOT of my more creative thinking went to die of inattention.

CHATTER #19

PARACHUTE CLUB-

RipChord Rock! What a hoot! Queen Street Kings and Queens or something. The late **Billy Bryans** assaulting his drum kit dressed in his finest Saharab gear, the husky, sexy vocals of **Lorraine Segato** in mufti on Congas, **Julie Massey's** sultry "**Innuendo**," and all the others made a truly tropical treat. Too bad they couldn't put it across stateside, they could have been huge.

They had a rather large (but not exclusive, cuz *I* was there, right?), Gay/Lesbian following, and watching the audience in **The Commodore** one night I found I didn't know where to look. A lot of their fans had their hair dyed colours not found in nature and the only way to tell anyone's true hair colour would be to have everyone drop their pants.

Reco- Parachute Club, "Rise Up," "Hot Hot Hot," "Innuendo"

PARKING-

One day, while filling out my Weekly Expenses, I noticed on the space for "Parking" that it said to "Explain Parking"; an odd question I thought, but, being a playa, I wrote: "Parking- the physical act of placing one's vehicle in a safe and stationary position, in order to visit Media in the Companys best interests, *now* can I have my Quarter?"

I read this to a roomful of convention attendees at the next opportunity and broke up most of the room. Accounting was NOT amused. Dour lot.

DOLLY PARTON-

Knock me over with a feather! If you googled "Nice Lady (that dresses like a hooker)," her picture would pop up. She flew the coop from Pigeon Forge straight to the top; it was Big Time or Bust for her and it turned out to be both. One of my career favorites. "**I Will always love you**," indeed.

One of Colonel Parker's tricks for writers or artists of more vulnerable stature. Elvis never wrote any of the songs that he was credited for on those early recordings, although *because* of his participation, the artists/writers allegedly profited *hugely*, as did Elvis and the colonel.

This type of maneuvering is not peculiar to the colonel, however; it still goes on, and it was the crafty, canny con carnie known as Col.Tom Parker who was none of those, said he wanted the rights for Elvis to record it, meaning in English, for HIMSELF for Elternity.

If he wasn't such a powerful Music biz figure he could have been a wrestler for all the arms he twisted, BUT Dolly would have NONE of it, she ***wouldn't*** give up her baby, and I'm proud of her for that alone.

Here we are with Dolly in January '85 backstage at the Coliseum presenting her with Platinum for her Christmas Album. L>R: Yours truly thinking..Helloo Dolly, the late Don Kollar-BMG Canada's Head Boob (Truer words…) and BMG Vancouver Branch Manager, the late Leagh Alden wearing what appears to be a cardboard suit.(Photo by Teurino Barbaro)

Reco- Dolly Parton, "Deportee (Plane Wreck at Los Gatos)," "I Will Always Love You"

PASSION (ERRING ON THE SIDE OF...)

Back in the day, talking 1970 AD, we didn't have the Communication Technology we have today; you had to have willpower (ok, sigh...WiPo, happy now?) to succeed. Basically, it was mail or the phone if you were out of town. One HAD to build relationships, the Music/Entertainment Biz was, and I hope, still is Relationship driven, not eDriven.

At **TPC/Quality**, one rule they had about Long Distance calls was...Don't take any and don't make any...so how to communicate? If I **REALLY** needed to talk to an out-of-town station, I'd call "Operator 6," which was code for RETURNING a call at the station's expense; by any means necessary.

King Lee/Victoria Times Colonist writer had a Music show on Radio CJVI Saturday nights and played **"Crow's "Don't Try to Lay no Boogie Woogie..."** as I wrote him a letter about it. It preceded (1970) the **Long John Baldry** version (1971); our band **Bigfoot** discovered it and played it, but we had NO idea how big it would become in others' hands. This was how you tried to start something.

Today there seems to be no end to available methods of technological communication: it's all electronic, internet, wireless, WiFi, Social or Anti-Social Media. Conspicuous in their absences are Psychics and Uri Geller, but at least they were people! Today, where is the one-to-one dialogue, the social interaction that goes beyond the fact you've gone to Asia on a trip, left the bath running and all your doors unlocked, on the internet for every footpad and cut-purse to read and take advantage of.

No.

Music, Art and Literature...are ***PASSION***, they are ***FEELING***, without that element, they wouldn't exist, and people **NEED** that stimulus, and altho I too use things like email for communication, sooner or later there has to be a human connection, a conversation, a beer, not an eBeer. This is all one dimensional, flat as piss on a plate. My long-suffering wife, who only wants good things for me (OK, explain GOOD), has threatened to get me a Twitter account, and God only knows what else to help me along the electronic highway (aka Cyberia)…Great! **MORE** shit to forget how it works, too much information. I used to tell my staff, as I was working on my exit strategy from BMG, do **NOT** just email somemediabody with a question upon whose answer untold millions of dollars and somebody's career rests; **show some respect, pick up the fucking phone**, y'know, that thing in your pocket you live on, that can pull down movies from other planets? Yeah, THAT thing, and **TALK** to somebody about it; otherwise, when people, stop needing people, REAL people, well…

All this striving for Integrity is an exercise in seeing that everyone gets what they need, if not what they want (Nod to Mick here). It takes being something of a Cerebral/Physical contortionist to achieve that, doing things Harry Houdini only dreamt of and sticking to your belief and commitment no matter how long it takes or how hard it seems. While you often work in ADVANCE of an Artist, NEVER put yourself AHEAD of the Artist, and **never say die.**

HUGH PICKETT-

Ran **Famous Artists**. He was an Old School Impresario, altho he eschewed that mantle, saying that **Sol Hurok (NY)** was the only *true* Impresario. For me, whether the Artist was **Paul Anka, Shirley Bassey** (he warned me to **NOT** go backstage as she was going Bitch-cakes) or **Monty Python's Flying Circus**. He **alway**s appreciated whatever help we could give.

As the Promoter, he could get a wee bit owly tho, like I'M not? I recall setting up Media for the Pythons and calling him to let him know what I'd done, and he told me, in no uncertain terms, that I couldn't do a THING without checking with him. Good thing I called, as that was *all* that *was* available to us at that moment.

I recall him NOT being a fan of neither **Brian Epstein** nor **Mick Jagger**, as he had to deal with both of them and their bands. He was also involved with the **Elvis** date in **Vancouver** as well, making it "Royalty" all around.

CHATTER #20

NESTOR PISTOR-

Oh my GOD. The things we did for him! The *For Prime Minister* LP promo was a Classic career moment.

Prior to my arrival at RCA, he got his big break performing in **Prince George** at their **Snow Golf** event as the scheduled comedian, **Arte Johnson** (Laugh In), couldn't make it.

Don Ast was an Entertainer of sorts out of Alberta, and started by clowning around and kidding his parents about their Ukrainian heritage; he'd put on an oversized overcoat, baggy pants with a rope belt and a train engineer's hat on sideways and go into his act. Rappers would call this a Throw Down; I think Nestor would call it a Throw Up. His accent was so thick you could make Borscht with it.

So Nestor Pistor, Ethno-Comic was born.

He did his stuff at the Snow Golf in Prince George, BC and for the princely price of a blank cassette tape, his first album was recorded; it sold THOUSANDS and THOUSANDS.

Nestor also fancied himself a Crooner, but as a singer, he was a good comedian.

So now I'm in the house, and his *Nestor Pistor For Prime Minister* record is coming out, and I put on my thinking crap...sorry, CAP, and away we go!

I purchase a bulk of train engineers caps, have "**Nestor Pistor for Prime Minister**" placards and banners made.

We bring him in for an in-store autograph signing in Surrey for the new LP and have the **RCA** staff parading around the YVR Terminal in the caps and signs, and here comes Nestor in character. I had hired my best friend Clayton's dad Nick to bring his **Cosco's Trucking & Bulldozing Dump Truck** up to the Terminal (pre-arranged with security and DOT), and there's the truck all draped with "NP for PM" banners, his Limo to Surrey.

Well…there's a lot of innocent people here, they meant well, they were mostly pissed or Pistored, if you will, I'm not dropping names here but that's either Elton John in the front centre or Bob Tait nicked his glasses.
(Photo by um…Blotto)

The In-Store was huge and we had the support of **Country 1130,** who did interviews and played Nestor's **"Wine-Stoned Plow-Boy"** (take THAT, Weird Al!) with apologies to Glenn Campbell and Jim Webb, who sang and wrote the original "**Rhinestone Cowboy**" and no doubt considered a restraining order for further attempts to murder their art. All this was followed by a show at the **Rootin' Tootin' Newton Inn**, which was sold out to the rafters!

I followed that shortly after with the Master Stroke (If I do say so, and this is me saying so) of having a Political Campaign Press Conference for Vancouver's Mainstream and Political watchdogs. This was set up at a Holiday Inn and catered by **Hunky Bill Konyk** (who also did Nestor's "World's Heavyweight Perogy Eating Contest" at **Treachers** that **Gene Kiniski** bowed out of), LOVE his food! I made certain there were NO knives or forks, this was true "finger food", and NO napkins, instead I had rolls of toilet paper on each table, and to wash it all down? Some of the worst/cheapest DRY Red wine money could buy!

And, using the old saw "Speaking on a Soap Box," I had a sturdy wooden one made, and stenciled "**Soap Box**" on it for the hard of thinking, for Nestor to Pontificate to the great unwashed masses upon. I still have that as a coffee table.

The results of all this were **AWESOME**: the Media "got it," ALL of it, and everyone had a GREAT time; we were **ALL OVER** the Political and Editorial pages, new ground for an entertainer, and were literally swimming in oceans of ink and acres of press.

For the time, it was a bit of Maverick marketing and it worked!

Possibly the **BEST** (Read; Most enjoyable) to me were the **Nestor Pistor** promos. I truly **LOVED** the "**Nestor Pistor for Prime Minister**" hijinx, the dump truck limo, the faux Press Conference for Vancouver's Political media (what a **HOOT!**), but the **BEST** had to be the "**World's Heavyweight Perogy Eating Championship**" contest at **Treachers Records** with Sundry Radio, Media and Music personalities weighing in on **Hunky Bill's** catering. I laughed for DAYS on end and sometimes still do at fully grown men being convinced they should do that, I needed Oxygen!

CHATTER #21

POWDER BLUES-

I signed them to **RCA**; one day, Tom called me and asked if I wanted the project...Um (nano second) **YES!**

Uncut was a dynamic record and success story. Tom had a friend do the deal with **Ed Preston**, but shortly after, **Bruce Allen** got involved, tore that puppy up, and made a better one! This is where I met my friend **Carlton Lee**, a wonderful guy.

It shud be noted that **CBS Canada** turned them down as "just another bar band." Oddly, the same thing **Dick Clark** said about the **Beatles,** which goes to show you: two wrongs don't make a **"Doin' it Right"**

One of my favorite shots of Tom Lavin, taken by Dee Lippingwell back in 1980. You'll note that's not Duris Maxwell on drums, this is a 2nd version of Powder Blues.

Reco- Powder Blues Band, "Doin' it Right," "Hear That Guitar Ring," "What've I Been Drinkin'"

Powder Blues Band "*UNCUT*" is a Classic album, Now go BUY a copy!

PRAIRIE OYSTER-

Incredible band, great people and working relationship, highly appreciative and not ashamed to say so.

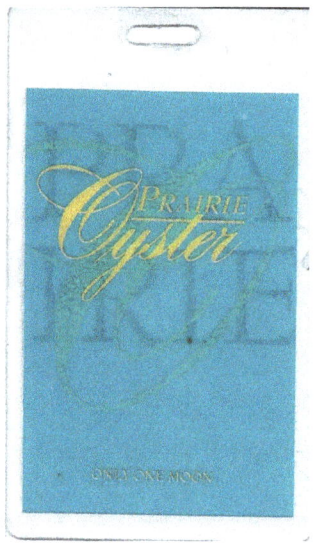

Reco- Prairie Oyster, "One Way Track," "Louisiette," "I Don't Hurt Anymore," "Something to Remember You By," "Unbelievable Love," "Black-Eyed Susan," and TOO many more

Prairie Oyster *w Rod McBeth (2nd from left), R's truly (Skunk-Face Killah) beside Russell 4th in back row, and BMG's Rona Goodman on far right*

This is one of the Best groups I ever worked with, true to the music and Country as a front porch. I'm proud to say that Russell DeCarle and I remain friends to this day, now that's something! Another group that's equally as great is Blue Rodeo that I never met or worked with but thoroughly enjoy listening to; Bonus, they BOTH Canadian!

THE POINTER SISTERS-

MORE tilting at windmills.

There were four sisters when I first started with this project, now there's only two left in the group with June's recent passing; she was the baby. I called them the "Pointy Sisters" for no other reason than I'm a bit silly.

I BELIEVED in them from the opening notes of their first single "**Salt Peanuts**," an old chestnut in itself. Nobody at Radio was listening, but I kept on from that to **Willie Dixon's "Wang Dang Doodle"** (it was SMOKIN'!), from the duet with the **Hoodoo Rhythm Devils** on their LP and beyond, once the "light" finally went on. Sometimes it's nice to be among the first rather than being lost among the many.

Rs truly backstage at the QET with 3 of the 4 Pointer Sisters back in their Blue Thumb days and as you can see, I was dressed for the occasion! Ah yes, we all used to 'dress' in those days.

Reco- Pointer Sisters' first LP with "Wang, Dang, Doodle," w Hoodoo Rhythm Devils, last track

PRESENTING-

I've Presented a few things over the years and most of them went smoothly.

A couple of others that stand out involve the **BC Country Music Association** (BCCMA); I was on the Board of Directors there for 2 years following my coming on board at RCA. The purpose was to keep an eye out for any outstanding talent that might be signable to our label and to lend a level of Music Business professionalism to the gaggle of Fans, Managers, and Bookers that made up most of the Board of Directors. Basically, it was a thankless task with a lot of infighting.

At that time, there was a thriving Country Music scene in the lower mainland; there were lots of Clubs and performers to fill their stages, and those people could make a living at this thing.

Along with expanding the **BCCMA** outside of the lower mainland, I also gave them their second Televised Awards show for continuity (after KVOS bailed after the first attempt) at **The Commodore** thru **Rogers**

Cable 4, a humble sophomore beginning, but an important step forward. My stepping down was a big step forward too; thank God for that!

Many years later, the **BCCMA** asked me to Present an Award, "**Entertainer of the Year**," I believe, at the Surrey Arts Center, a proposition to which I agreed after I twisted their arm for a ticket for my wife, huh.

I did make an "entrance," along with my wife Lynne and friend Richard Watt, in a Stretch Limo, which stood out amongst the Pickup Trucks and Wal-Mart Parking Lot Beaters.

So, I go backstage to prep, which consists of asking a lot of people where I go on, and run into then-Politico **Jim "Lefty" Nielsen** with a brand-new shiner, a result of cuckolding some poor bastard until he came home unexpectedly. He once was the **MD** at **Radio CJOR** in Vancouver when they played Country Music, waaay before **CKWX** picked up the reins.

Now it's Showtime and I'm (mis)directed to the WRONG SIDE OF THE STAGE, and then pushed toward the correct side. I have to pick my way thru wires and cables strewn about the stage in the dark and in my unlit rush, trip and fall over them. Picking myself up by the seat of my own pants I finally make it to the podium, say "Hello," tell everyone what a great "trip" I had, and read the Nominations, and stop, then tell the audience that I'd **LOVE** to tell them who won but I don't have the envelope, which is suddenly and sharply jabbed into the palm of my hand (is that blood?). Amidst **GALES** of laughter from the audience, I exit, not to return for many years; that was in the Mid '90s.

In 2006, I was called upon to be a judge for a BCCMA Talent showcase, which would serve as an "opening act" for the headlining **Johnny Reid** at the **Cloverdale Fairgrounds**; *those* people put on a good show, some were exceptional, especially the ones that bent the genre to showcase their talent. Some were near Classic/Operatic, and one girl in particular knocked everyone's hat off, which is fine, after all, it's just Music.

In 2011, they called back.

Whole new crew, they've always been volunteers.

This time they asked if I would induct **Jess Lee** into the BCCMA **Hall of Fame**; they wanted to give me all kinds of background on him, but as I signed him (**Midnite Rodeo Band**), I begged off, telling them I knew him so well I knew his real name, but wouldn't tell. As they readily agreed to ticket Lynne this time, I agreed.

It was at the Red Robinson Theatre that year, at The Boulevard Casino in Coquitlam, nice room, good audio, lots of video screens.

Showtime: after my intro I tell the audience the story of how Ed insisted I see his new Vocal partner, and I was impressed with his pipes, he had a voice that would make Lefty cry and Haggard sigh and enuff bad habits to make him a star! And he WAS a star with MRB, and after that struck out on his own, and is comfortable with the success he has. I wish him all the best, and for him to keep his hands off my wallet and my wife.

Tab ahead to 2016...I was called by the **BCCMA** to inquire if I might accept being inducted into their **Country Music Hall of Fame**, and I, hoping I wasn't being pranked, said **YES!** At Light Speed, and I was indicted by none other than **Jess Lee!**

Shooter- Lynne Ramsay

I participated again in 2017 by presenting their **Producer of the Year** award, video link here:

https://youtu.be/jPrd7yAhHc0

For your further amusement, here is the Media ePressR sent out in advance of the event:

Feb 5/16

Media ePressR(Ray Ramsay BCCountry Music Hall of Fame) The Grandstanding SOB Version

THE LAD IN LADNER TO COUNTRY MUSIC ALL OF FAMEHALL OF FAME!

Ray Ramsay, long time Music Industry Veteran who signs off communications as "The Lad in Ladner,", and has an Umbrella company called "ALadinLadner" for his Music, Literary and Marketing pursuits, will be inducted into BC's Country Music Hall of Fame on April 10th.

The **BCCMA** is proud to announce its 2016 Hall of Fame inductees: First, the four Rs of this indictment- **Ray Ramsay, Red Robinson**, then the venerable **Denny Eddy, Laurie Thain, Mike Norman, Farmer's Daughter, Gerry Leiske, Tammy Ray, Redd Volkaert, and John McLaughlin.**

Ray secured his first job with a Record company largely, he suspects, as a way of having him stop phoning and badgering them. He started on April 1, 1968, an auspicious date for this April Fool, to be followed by his hire date later at **RCA**, and throughout his tenure, over 36 years with Record labels alone, along with Artists of all Music Genres, he worked with the best and sometimes Legendary Country Stars Canada and America had to offer.

Grizzly Ramsay, as he is known to his Music Buds and Readers, was hired by RCA Canada at their Vancouver Branch the same day Elvis died (Nice start!), Aug. 16, 1977, by the late, great John Ford (who went on to head RCA Canada in Toronto, and RCA U.S. out of New York). Once settled (this is MY chair?), John encouraged him to join the Board of the BC Country Music Association to continue to offer Music Biz experience and guidance to the fledgling organization (which consisted largely and loosely of Performers, Booking Agents, Managers, and fans), as well as to keep an ear out for any promising performers or writers that may interest RCA.

Once on Board, he decided to raise it above the seminal Fan Club level by enlisting Rogers Cable 4 TV (KVOS TV having bailed after their debut awards show) to cover that year's Annual "**Danny Awards**" show at The Commodore, one of their first Televised events. He topped that the following year by convincing CKVU-TV (Now Citytv) to cover that awards show.

As the lower mainland was saturated with showcase events by largely the same performers, Ramsay decided, along with former Board member and Country Music aficionado **Richard Watt** of **Treachers Records**, as it was the *BC* **Country Music Association,** to set up the first out-of-town showcase in the Central Okanagan City of **Kelowna** with Guest Artists "**Ed & Jess.**" This was Ed Molyski and Jess Lee, who were the heart and soul of the **Midnite Rodeo Band** and were later signed to RCA (Huh!). This foray into the "outer" earned the BCCMA a lot of prestige and awareness and bolstered the membership significantly.

The venue for this event was **Weninger's Post House** in Kelowna, later to be renamed **Ronnie Prophet's Ranch House** and finally, being unprofitable (cough), simply, "**Closed.**"

In 1980, Ray staged, nearly single-handedly (A little Help??), the first **Ray McAuley** Memorial concert, "**A Tribute to Ray McAuley**," on a Monday night, Feb. 11 at the Rootin' Tootin' **Newton Inn**. It was so sold out, you had to go outside to change your mind. Aside from honoring Ray, who had died the previous year of a Brain Aneurism, this also served to launch **Ray McAuley & Wild County's** Posthumous LP *Memories*. The main band featured Ray's writer and Six String Savant, **Ed Molyski**, and Country

Music Future Star, the aforesaid **Jess Lee**. All the proceeds went to the BCCMA; pretty generous, eh?

Ray and his long-suffering "Keeper Wife" Lynne moved from Steveston in 2002 to settle here (is that MY chair?) in the Steaming Metropolis of **Ladner** Sur Mer (There be DOGS here!). In spite of repeated attempts to have him tarred, feathered and run out of town on Light Rail, they have since relocated again to White Rock in 2019.

He has always stood for his Artist and is NEVER averse to engaging in a Classic "Bumstead/Dithers" brawl (preceding the UFC by miles) if he felt a Radio Station was stiffing his Artist for airplay on records that even Vincent Van Gough could hear were hits, notably **Radney Foster** or **The Tractors** (yes, even they had their detractors). He was proven to be Right more often than not, but he preferred to be more timely and profitable than morally correct.

In summation, a quote from the Lovable Curmudgeon..."G*RRRRRR*! No! Not that! This!"

I have been blessed & honored to work in this bidness, with some truly Great Music people and artists over the length & breadth of my checkered and speckled participation. My role in the local Country scene was just something I was able to get involved with to try and raise it above being the Best Pumpkin in the patch to Artists/Writers of considerable consequence (I TOLD you there'd be Consequences!), so in closing, THANK YOU for this honor, and NO, I have NO idea if Glen Campbell wears a wig so please stop asking (whistling here...Happy Trails...)

CHATTER #22

PRESS PALS-

Tom Harrison, Kerry Gold, John Mackie, Stuart Derdeyn and the Humorous and Poignant **Dan Murphy** whose **"101 Things you can do with a Severed Penis"** book is a real slice (sorry!), and not to forget, **The Victoria Times Colonist's Mike Devlin**; all old school, all good people. Got along so well with them, Pacific Press honored me with a going away broadside, something they only do for staffers, which hangs matted and mounted in my office, the Cistern Chapel.

Promo Monkey: My Life as a BellHop in the Waldorf Hysteria

133

Tom Harrison, my friend from his **Radio CiTR (UBC)** days has a WICKED sense of humor and never fails to crack me up. He took direct aim at his Nemesis **David Bendeth** once when reviewing a record David produced by a group on **CBS** called **"Cats Can Fly."** Tom's review was: "But Turkeys can't!" If David's name was on a record, it might as well be "Mud" with the Dailies in this market.

I cannot forget my pal Rootin' Tootin' **Steve Newton**, who must have dragged his guitar to nearly every show we had to get it autographed, and who became the unwitting target for eternal revenge from **Mötley Crüe** for catching them out for something or other. At one show, they found out what seat he had, but he wisely wasn't in it when they had somebody go up to it with a bucket of urine, **YIKES!** So is it better to be pissed off, or pissed on?

ED PRESTON-

Smilin' Ed. He ran **RCA Canada** with a smile and generous hand, a true Professional. Glad to have known him. Went on to handle the careers of **Roger Whittaker** and **Carroll Baker**, I wish him happiness and health.

SUZI QUATRO-

I told *everybody* "the Bitch was Back!" And forth; I tried, and then she left. While I was involved with the promotion of her records (while we had her), I didn't get a chance to meet or work with her, altho she did open for **John Mayall** at **UBC** one time, and John was with my label, **Blue Thumb**. She also came from a musical family; her sister was in **Fanny**, one of the premier All-Girl Rock bands (on **Casablanca**), and her brother **Michael** was a keyboardist/songwriter that had an LP out on one of the labels I repped. Michael also played a large part in Suzi's fortunes, as he was the one that got her hooked up with UK Producer **Mickey Most**, and from there to management by **Chas Chandler**, formerly of **the Animals**; Chas also had an early hand in **Jimi Hendrix's** English tenure

RADIO-

Music Directors: They were Radio's front lines against Promo Reps; they sift out what those people have to say and prepare a kind of research buffet for the weekly meeting: Hmm, a grain of truth, divide by three, add several grains of salt if not the entire lick and…

Benoit DuFresne was the worst; he was a NICE guy BUT he could say NO! in TWO languages, not fair!

Another MD, when I brought the station a re-issue of a David Bowie LP so they'd have a clean copy, but really thinking I wanted to get it some airplay (it's an *OLD* record!), looked at me in all seriousness and said, "I think this town's all Bowied-out, either that or I'm full of shit," to which I replied, "either way, I think you're right." He never even blinked.

Yet another told me, after one listen to **Whitney Houston's "I Will Always Love You**," that it would do okay' (lower case) at Adult Contemporary Radio Stations; open mouth, change feet.

Here's a Kodak moment…The Fox gave *ME* a plaque! And these guys knew what they were doing; see **"Everlast"**

ON-AIR CONTESTS FROM THE PROMO DOMO:

I was responsible for some pretty crazy promotions thru the years; I inflicted 2 on **CKPG/Prince George**, both Christmas LPs, both involving animals and no small amount of cruelty to the captive Radio audiences; there was "**Meowy Christmas, The Jingle Cats**," and the **Jingle Dogs'** "**Bark the Halls with Howls of Bowser**" I *think* it was, and both had these poor animals calling (for the SPCA, no doubt) along to carols.

ON-AIR FARE:

I first met my old Radio bud **Tom** (who went by the Nom de Air 'Jeffries') at **CKPG**, and I know his and many others' REAL names, having kept them in a book. Quite often these DJs would move from market to market and you'd only know they were in town by seeing their "Wanted" poster in the post office.

Unfortunately, **CKPG** had a very serious moment of "Dead Air" when the Prince George Rapist was having his way, as it was their **Morning Man** who was arrested while he was on-air by the RCMP! Good for beratings but not so good for Ratings.

For the record, it WASN'T Tom.

Meeting an out-of-town Announcer for the first time was always interesting, as they have voices about 6 foot 5 inches, but when you come face-to-face (only an expression as I am 6' 1") a lot of them are about 5 foot nothing in their stalking feet.

Many DJs try to expand their talents to TV, but it's more of a gap than people may think, and not everyone makes it, as, altho they have the VOICE, well, there's an expression in the Broadcast Medium, "A good FACE for Radio".

Ed Bain from **100.3 The Q,** Victoria's Breakfast show, comes to mind as being very successful in making the transition and STAYING. He's still one of the funniest **Morning Drive** people I have heard; I've nearly driven off the road reacting to some of the things he says AND he also does the **CHEK 6** News/Weather. I've no idea when Ed has time to sleep, hmmmm and he doesn't seem to AGE either, maybe he's a Vampire? A lot of bite, at any rate.

There was the **Crash Test Dummies** promo for the "**Worms Life**" CD that had me & Lynne up at **4 AM** and visiting Morning Radio shows to offer the DJs a container of Live **Dew Worms** in which was embedded the single; the Early Bird gets the…poor Lynne following me around as I wore a worm sock puppet on my right hand and a chicken head mask (which

Lynne created for me) thru the burbs right to downtown Vancouver, where there was apparently a Stoic's Convention, as a lot of people just stared blankly; maybe they weren't up yet, poor things, but Lynne got it all on video!

Some of the other Nut-bar Promos included a **Crash Test Dummies** promo for their first CD **"Ghosts That Haunt Me"** on **CFJC/TV-Kamloops** focused on the characters in the video for what would eventually be a **MASSIVE** Hit, **"The Superman Song,"** where a group of individuals were attending the Funeral of **him** almost all are former Superheros & Crimefighters. The contest hinged on viewers writing in and identifying who those characters were, and the answers, which I still have, are freaking HOWL-arious! Those people were having too much fun at once in somewhat, if not drastically, altered states.

Another time, **St Patrick's Day** was at hand, and I gave **The Fox's Larry & Willy** a 10 lb bag of potatoes to give away with the (Irish BAND) **The Chieftains**' new release, one spud/record at a time; I laughed so hard I wept. I believe this was the album with a lot of guest artists on it, including what sounded like a highly impaired **Rolling Stones** (they drove over to Ireland with their own Bar in tow) and perfectly butchered their own song **"Satisfaction,"** which shud have been credited as "DIS-Satisfaction".

ON ERR:

Slee you in Court!-A quick lesson in protecting your Brand.

This happened on a Toronto Radio Station during the Breakfast show.

John Sleeman (Sleeman's Brewery) was in the studio to discuss a new product, and unbeknownst to him, the Announcer Humbly set up a Beer tasting. John was offered a Beer purported to be the Announcer's Home Brew; John tried it, and said that it wasn't bad, but wasn't great, when the announcer said Sorry! That was YOUR Beer, mine is over here!

In one motion, Mr. Sleeman rose and left the studio and canceled ALL of his advertising on THE ENTIRE STATION CHAIN on his way out.

The Announcer was fired.

So, while **John Sleeman** laughed all the way to the bank, the Radio Station Management were left to cry in their Beer.

NICK JAGUAR:

... on being fitted for a Law Suit...

Years ago, when **CKLG/LG73** was the reigning Pop 40 Powerhouse in Vancouver, there was a time when they may have been TOO well off, as there seemed to be a complacency lapse while minding the Evening show.

It's a given that listenership would drop off precipitously after 6PM with the Afternoon rush over and home. This show had a team of two pranking young guys, who, having been relegated to that time slot, missed the buzz of the BIG contest announcements during the day, sooooo they decided to take to the air and give away a...**Jaguar**, yeah.

They huffed and they puffed and they plugged and they pitched the contest and the phone lines lit right up!

This went on for about a week, I think, and then the day came to announce a winner, and HOOO Boy, was the lady excited to have won; I think she was levitating, and if you can do THAT, what do you need with a car?

...and then they revealed that the car was, in fact, a toy, **a Dinky Toy**, or today we'd have called it a Hot Wheels model, uh huh.

There was a brief pause while the winner consulted her litigious husband, who was a...**Lawyer**, and who huffed and puffed and threatened to blow the station down unless they came up with a **REAL** car.

This caused a series of Brown Trouser moments among the announcers, management and owners, but it all ended well for the contest winner, now in possession of a spanking new **FULL SIZE ejag.**

I suppose the Moral here may be that if you let your (unsupervised) on-air talent run amok, you should consider putting them on VERY short leashes if you don't want to be paying for very expensive high-end Sports Cars; it's the leash you can do.

RCA-

At **RCA** you were always in the **Dog House, Nippers!** It was a GREAT home.

A lot of people think the dog's name is Victor; those same people put their shoes and socks on in that order.

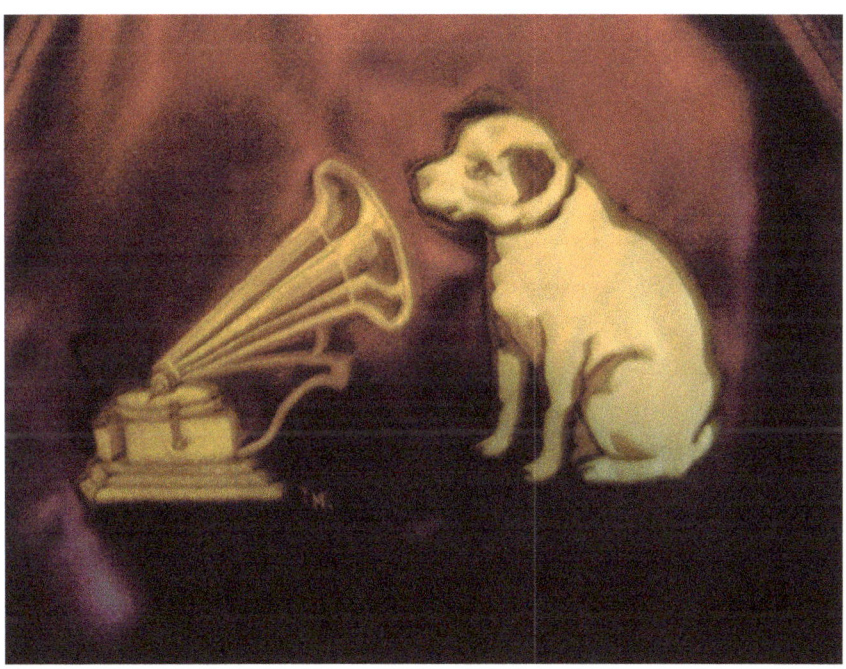

RASCALZ-

Are you freaking KIDDING ME!? These guys were so much work they were a career by *themselves*. Sometimes I didn't know if I was a Promotions guy or a Fireman!

Hey! Do I smell like weed?! No, you smell like a Metric Tonne of weed.

Our resident Rap Group Rascalz were …Rascals.

They were doing a show at a club in Victoria and had us set up an in-store signing there at **HMV** in co-operation with their manager, who looked after the Technical side. Lynne and I went over for the in-store (she was **BMG Van Office Coordinator**), which was good, as it got out of control quickly, unusual for a Rap act (cough!).

When we got to the store, we found the wheels falling off, as there was no equipment for a mini-set. After a rousing round of finger pointing (at us) and name calling (us again), the **HMV** store manager produced the Tech list, and the **Rascalz** manager had taken great care to not include *any* of the required equipment on it (Good Weedership?). The good thing is HMV manager got the required stuff from a contact of his in a trice and the show was on!

While the short delay waiting for the equipment set-up went on, the store was filling up with fans and shoplifters, and when it was a go, Lynne and I, along with some HMV store staff, formed the good old Flying Wedge around the group and got them to the stage on time. Voila! Order out of chaos.

RASCALZ.2:

Their 2nd Album "*Global Warning*" (1999) was about to Pop, and I set up as robust a Media schedule as possible to launch it. Their 1st Album "*Cash Crop*" (1997) had done reasonably well, but didn't garner local Top 40 airplay; there seemed to be tension between the group and **Z95** from the get-go. I thought "**Dreaded Fist**" was a good track, still do, but I couldn't get it over.

Reco- Rascalz, "Dreaded Fist"

THIS was a new day and a new Album and one of the Prime Media interviews I got was on **BCTV**, hosted by former Z95 Music Director **Zack Spencer.**

I took this promo campaign and this TV interview to be a fresh start, everything else, water under the bridge, we were going for it this time. The **Rascalz** didn't quite see things the same way and took this as an opportunity to flay the Radio Station alive as the focus of the interview and their ire. Yeah, that sound behind me IS Jesus weeping.

This wasn't helping. I can understand their frustration but this was neither the time nor place for revenge.

Fortunately, I had a good relationship with Zack and got him to see our perspective and delete the vitriol against the station and focus on the new music, and say no more, the interview went to air; a pretty good piece, just as the record was dropping; everything was coming up Roses…

…sorry, Rancid. Unfortunately, I didn't know about a rather incendiary interview they'd done with a tertiary newspaper, again raging against the station, which the Radio Station had the courtesy to show me when I brought their new single in…sigh, some days are diamonds, some days are C4.

RAY'S IDEA ORPHANAGE-

This was a file I kept of ideas, some pretty darn GOOD ideas, that, in the end, nobody else gave a shit about. I heard a lot ABOUT the ideas, but rarely saw one put into action. The "*FoxWorthy*" sampler and the ***Dave Matthews Band Sampler*** are two exceptions. The rest, I'll say it again, basically died of inattention, and we might have made some extra $$$$, who's to say.

ROY HENNESSY/CKLG-

Lord, he had the patience of Job, and that allowed me to grow; the shit he had to listen to from me!

REGGAE MUSIC –

Bob Marley, Toots, Jimmy Cliff, so many, so good. Worked **HARD** to bring this to the public attention and educate retailers, then Eric Clapton did "**I Shot the Sheriff**" and everyone went Oh THAT'S Reggae! NO it's NOT, that's POP! You HAVE to hear the real thing! My daughter Vanessa benefited greatly from all this exposure to music, and she liked Reggae and may possibly have been the only four year old to know the words to songs like "**Pressure Drop**."

BILL REITER-

An R&B buddy. Signed him for "**Injun Jim Blues**" for **Quality** (on **Skyline**). The title references how the media of the time referred to Jim Thorpe a native American and Olympiad contender who endured tragedy after travesty at the hands of white people.

Then Bill came around with his *Doctor Bundolo* LP and I signed that to **RCA**, a second Monty Python Experience. He has a **GREAT** sense of humor; one day I was taking him to lunch and he wanted to go for fish & chips, saying his Producer, Kenny, was with us, and, being English, could show us how to eat them.

Also, when Bill went to Russia for some reason (never worked in a Salt Mine, been to a Gulag?) he brought me back a copy of the **Russian National Anthem** on vinyl; I'm still at a loss for words and I still have it. I was hoping for a copy of the song the Kremlin put out (at gunpoint no doubt) to quell the fever for the **Fab Four** (and all Invasions British) and instigate their own brand of Lenin-mania, which works well if you *say it*, but not so well on paper; the song was "**Don't Be Such a Beatles**" (Could have been a big hit for **Nestor Pistor**!) and that's TRUE. While the Russian National Anthem doesn't get much above a dirge, the flip side picks up with "**The Volga Boatman**"; Rock and Row. Yeah.

RED ROBINSON-

I started off listening to Red as a youth in bed on my Crystal Rocket Radio, got into the Biz and met and worked with him, even guesting on his show a time or two. Ensured he got some respect and dignity for his work with our label, especially on the *"Elvis: A Canadian Tribute"* CD, instead of just a free copy in the mail. Actually, I got to present him with gold plaques **TWICE;** once for the vinyl and the other for the CD. The second one (here) was presented on **KVOS-TV Bellingham, Washington, USA**, Vancouver being about 85% of its viewers, and wouldn't you know, Red had a show on it; why put a record out and not **DO** something about it. Good friends.

*Here we are: Rs truly giving Red his just desserts for his contribution on the "**Elvis: A Canadian Tribute**" CD at the now defunct Hard Rock Café in Vancouver during a taping of Red's KVOS/TV Bellingham USA show, in 1999 I believe.*
*Photo by Dee Lippingwell

RESPECT-

Like in some Italian/Sicilian family organizations, Respect works wonders; I know it did in the Music Biz of yore. It gets things done cooperatively, but Respect, is earned; no job title will get any instant real Respect without empathetic cooperation behind it. Without that, you're like **General Custer** in an Arrow shirt.

It's nice to be liked, but with a lot of people, I could do without being liked if I was respected for getting things done. A side order of "Please," "Thanks" and follow-up to complete the plate.

Seeing somebody do a good job to whatever possible degree of success in a forthright manner deserves Respect, or even flattery if one can duplicate or elevate an outcome, as happened to me in one particular instance.

Building good relationships, establishing a welcome rapport, working cooperatively and in collaboration with others of regard, be it a competitor or contact, can move mountains.

I was regarded by some in our Head Office as the "Emperors Clothier," and some were reluctant to approach me about the progress of their projects Bcuz they knew I would tell them the real deal and not necessarily what they wanted to *believe* was happening. There was no Moondance wishing & hoping, just pure Rayality, mixed with a healthy dose of effort for forward momentum; it was straight up doin' or ruin.

Some projects were like pushing a rock uphill, and some rocks just won't roll, but I found the most satisfying projects were the HARD ones, not just sitting around, going thru the motions until American Radio/Media "broke" the ice for you. Tenacity and palpable Persistence win the day. It's a combination of Inspiration and Perspiration. **Be driven.**

There's not much that can't be done; add a pinch of "**Desire**" and if there isn't presently an opportunity, then...create one. Use the relationships you built; nobody does much successfully on their own hook. Share the passion and seal the deal & together, the reward and pleasure of the achievement.

Amen…Ding! Ding!...class dismissed.

CHATTER #23

RAYNAISSANCE-

A rebirth, my musical one anyway.

Little Richard got it started and I continued on, first picking up playing the drums with a couple pointers from a friend and on a practice pad I made in the basement. I took "lessons" from some of the greatest drummers in the Pop world, people like **Al Jackson Jr.**, **Roger Hawkins**, **Ringo**, **Charlie Watts**, and a plethora of the other Rock and R&B beaters put on the records I would practice to.

Me, on stage with **Bigfoot**, *just GIVIN'R!*
Work & play, same thing.
Shooter- Wayne Bailey

Next, I went on to learn guitar with a bit of direction from my friend and band mate **Down Home Jerome**/Jerry Walliser. I would practice every day on a solid body Electric guitar I borrowed from a friend, altho it had no Amp, so I'd have to really focus to hear myself, which likely contributed to my plodding, pedestrian, lead handed, ham-fisted style (Top THAT, Eric!). It served me well enuff to write some songs, some with Jerome and some on my own.

What really got me on the back-beaten path were some high school classmates that had a band, but no name at that point, and I thought they were pretty good. This was **Steve Cropley, Howard Ho, Tim Ng**, and I'm embarrassed to say I've forgotten the drummer's name, which is odd, as the drummer is always the first person I take notice of, so my apologies if ever he reads this. So, we talked and I would be their Manager, and altho at that time I really had NO idea what that truly meant, I had the enthusiasm for them.

At one rehearsal, I noticed that "**Needles & Pins**" was probably their best song, so I said "go with that," and they did. And now they're the **Needles & Pins**, and I designed a logo for them using two Guitars and a Pick and crafted the script inside those, not bad for the time. I think I still have that original drawing somewhere, as I was quite proud of how clever it was.

That was my High School Music Biz career; **David Letterman** would later say that the Music Business is like High School with money, and later I would find that he was right!

It would still be a couple more years of detours before I finally landed a job in the Music Industry, largely, I suspect as a means to have me stop phoning them; I was determined. My family wanted me to have a nice safe job as clerk, a fucking CLERK! Somewhere like The Bay, but I was having **NONE** of that, I was doing this my way (A clerk!). BUT, I was IN, and it was Music, it was *always* about the Music...

KENNY ROGERS-

More career starts than a cat has lives. I worked with him so often I thought I'd start looking like him, and I did. He's the master of the short conversation; if you're still talking to him after two minutes and thirty seconds, you're talking to yourself. Kenny is gone, tennis anyone?

1st Photo is 1985 at the Pacific Coliseum. Photo by Teurino Barbaro and L>R: BMG Canada's version of Andre the Giant, Pres Don Kollar (They are both deceased now) R2, Dolly, Kenny, and Leagh Alden (also Past Tense) in that same Goddam suit! Hmmm, maybe he's still wearing it?

2nd Photo is 1983, same venue, Photo by Kent Remember: Leagh, Me and Heavy Metal Kenny in the middle.

ROMEO'S DAUGHTER-

"Crying in the Back Seat" was the single and I decided to spice things up by delivering the singles in a plastic bag full of diced cooking Onions. Yep! Big ol' flavorful me. Yes, there were tears, and MDs throwing chairs thru windows to get air. Good Fun! No airplay!

DIANA ROSS-

I *didn't* call her **"Miss Ross"** and I *did* look her in the eye, both eyes actually, she had two, I don't do Kowtow.

I remember when **RCA** signed her and the album graphics were being passed around and ideas for Promo were being called for; as it was a head shot of her with what appeared to be an animal skin, I suggested having a contest to send a winner on Safari to be eaten by a wild animal, but it was rejected as being "too costly," Hmm...the trip or the lawsuit?

The first time she played Vancouver (post-signing) she had more costume changes than God has spells, and backstage access was limited. At that time, I had a back injury and that night it was so painful I swear my back was speaking in tongues, but I KNEW I HAD to meet a high maintenance artist like this or face a New York hotline meltdown the next morning.

So, there I was backstage at last, there's her dressing room and there's the limo, and I station myself between the two and here she comes, on the run! I step in front of her and hand her my card, give a quick intro, and she stops, gives me a BIG hug and says she's sorry but she has to go! I reply, that's OK Diana, I have that effect on women, she laughs and leaps into the limo, and our happiness is complete, if not Supreme.

*This is 1981 at the Pacific Coliseum. Leagh, Me and Lady Di in the middle. If you read Dee's book "**First Three Songs…No Flash**" THIS is the shot she was talking about and this is the 1st time I worked with her; the Limo intervention incident was the 2nd.*
Shooter- Dee Lippingwell

CHATTER #24

RAYCOLLECTING-

When **Arthur "Big Boy" Crudup**, the writer of **"That's All Right,"** **Elvis Presley's** first hit single, was asked how well he was doing after the song went to number 1, he had the remarkable response…That Arnold Preston never gave me nuthin!

ROCK-A-BILLY-

We had an artist, **Robert Gordon**, on **RCA** in 1979 with some degree of success. He had a tour date at The Commodore with British Guitar wunderkind **Chris Spedding**, who we believe sold at least half the tickets.

Robert did an afternoon Press Conference at the venue and his image was quite camera-ready; in fact, this photo captures him perfectly and is one of my favorite pics, even tho Robert as a person wasn't one of my favorite picks.

One of my all-time favorite photos; Robert Gordon during a Press Conference @ The Commodore. No Photog credit found.

The show was well attended, and to follow it, we had arranged an in-store autograph session across the street at **"Glenn's Records,"** at which Robert balked last minute, insisting he require some "refreshment," the Real Thing in a way. I was SO pissed at this being held for ransom (What, you're Chuck Berry now?) I told him in the most unmistakable terms that if he didn't get his ass across the street RIGHT FUCKING NOW, he would never sell another record in *this* town!

Soooo, across the street we go, meet the Great Unwashed Public, sign some records, and away we go, almost everybody is happy, he is free to go powder his nose and I've never seen nor spoken to him since; works for me.

ROYALTY-

When I was with **TPC/Quality**, we had **"The QUEEN of Soul," Aretha Franklin,** on **Atlantic,** and I and a roomful of others waited in vain for her at a pre-concert reception once.

When I got to **RCA**, their biggest act Elvis, "The KING of Rock & Roll" dropped dead the day I was hired.

Another "Queen of Rock & Roll", **Little Richard,** changed my life forever with one listen to **"Good Golly Miss Molly."**

Otis Redding was, to me, "The KING of Soul" still is.

My Aunt Vera was dressmaker to **Queen Elizabeth** for a time in London. The irony here is that while she was stitching Lizzie's knickers, my Mother's side of the family is actually *related* to the Royal Family (I could do with some Royalties myself about now!), and while he's not Royalty per se we are also related to John Quincy Adams, the 6th President of the United States; no shit.

I suppose I should add that I have been, and p'raps still am, a ROYAL Pain-in-the-ass to any number of people (It's a Gift): you may kneel in my presence and rejoice in my absence.

Now, I am reminded of an act on **RCA**, just around the time I was considering Raytiring, by the name of **"Kings of Leon"** that **RCA** had the foresight and good sense to sign in a bidding war. I met them when they played **"Richards"** eons of Leons ago. The band was made up of the Followill clan, whose father, a self-styled Fire & Brimstone preacher, was on a first name basis with His nibs, God, and his first born, The King of Kings.

We should have had Father Followill promote the band (to the Heavens?) in Vancouver as we sure as Hell didn't have a prayer here ourselves, nope.

In spite of impressive U.S. Radio activity and them just blowing up everywhere else in general, Rock Radio in Vancouver was having another **Dave Matthews, Tool, Crash Test Dummies, David Gray** Blind-in-one-ear-and-can't-see-out-of-the-other moment. I DO hope they've gotten over themselves since I left.

SANTANA-

Was hands down one of the NICEST people I met, more concerned about what was happening with YOU than his record!

Again, THANK GOD for The Q, nothing wrong with THEIR ears! In Vancouver **NOBODY** would play him at first, claiming it was the "other" station's record, and at this point I told PDs and MDs they were the reason I wasn't allowed to carry a fire-arm, not to shoot them but myself after listening to all their bullshit. And then, it clicked, the record, not the gun, and was on the air for over a YEAR!

Carlos & Buds: BMG Buds backstage at GM Place, now Rogers Arena in 2000

L>R R2 (2nd Fiddle to Carlos), Him, (Bk) Shane Carter/BMG TO (The man who would be King and IS), BK Steve Simon/BMG TO (Ft) All BMG staff Miss Catherine Wong, Christine Woo, (Bk) Matthew Pinch, (Ft) Tanya-Temp, (Bk) Troy Dickson (A good catch), M2/Mike Moreau, The Lovely Lisa, (Bk) Keith Porteous in full scowl, Dale Robertson

PLEASE DON'T PLUMP THE PRODUCE!-

What?!

Stay with me here...now this is a bit weird. Not sure how many people at the Ladner Grocery Behemoth (Savor food, or something) know about the background to what is pretty much their theme song, BUT I do.

The lyric is the chorus of a big hit record I had while I was with **Quality/TPC** by the **Andrea True Connection**, the track being "**More, More, More.**" The thing is, Andrea True was a **Porn Star**, and this is a Family oriented food store!

Nobody checked?

Here we are, still in the grocery store; I also had a record (***Benihana***) by **Marilyn Chambers** on **Roulette Records (in my collection)**; fittingly enough and **SHE was a Porn Star too!**

It got so I had to wear rubber gloves to handle my record collection!

Now Marilyn became famous for her appearance, albeit briefly, on the cover of **Ivory Snow** detergent boxes (just wash your Sins away!) until somebody wised up; so, NOT as pure as the driven snow?

What next, **John Holmes** singing **"Big Bad John"** for a sausage company?

Over at **Saveway**, they aren't as much Musical as just creepy…ingredients for Life. So what, you're **Victor Frankenstein** now?

BEV SHANNON-

The Beav! ...I'm Wally

My VERY good friend who savors my every discomfort (tell me about being chased by angry wild dogs again Ray! I LOVE that story!) and who supported me through two record labels, TPC/Quality and RCA, while squeezing in an unappreciated stint at **Capitol** before I hired her away to some dignity.

She also got me involved with **BC Children's Hospital** and her **Wigs for Kids BC** campaigns, which I've been contributing to since 2006, raising awareness and money for kids and their families battling Cancer, most of it Pro Bono, Sonny's poorer brother.

*Here's my GOOD friend Bev (The Beav!) and her hubby Rick (Bobaloo!) with me at the "***Let's Throw Raymond from the Gravy Train***" Raytirement Party at The Roxy. Right after this photo was taken, Rick mistakenly thinking my shirt was on fire, rolled me on the ground until **I** was out!*
Shooter- Dee Lippingwell

BILLY JOE SHAVER-

For using the unword 'wudn't' in a song; anyone who can do THAT...

SHELLY SIEGEL-

A Mensch and a **Mushroom** grower. Made and WAS **Mushroom Records** the 1st **Heart** Album "*Dreamboat Annie*" and then **Chilliwack**, "*Dreams, Dreams, Dreams*" and…he also broke these in the U.S. where they *smell* a hit. He was a dynamo, and then he died. After that, there wasn't much Mushroom anymore.

CHATTER #25

POCO / EAGLES-

I am reminded by a recent **Eagles** concert in Vancouver that I once had an association with them, or one of them at least.

I was always a fan of their music, as I was of **Joe Walsh** in his **James Gang** days (**Funk 49, Ashbury Park,** and the Rockstended version of **Howard Tate's** R&B hit "**Stop!**")

I am **deeply** touched by "**Last Resort**" from the *Hotel California* LP, as the first time I heard that was right after I found out that my friend Brian had jumped off the Granville Street bridge onto Beach Ave and killed himself.

So young and SO troubled, we didn't see that coming.

Sadly, exactly a month, to the day later, his wife did the SAME thing, same place.

I never fail to feel the emotion whenever I hear that song, even today.

I first heard **Poco's** "**Rose of Cimarron**" on (then) **CKLG-FM**, and being impressed with the sound, Country without the Bumpkin.

My last encounter with them, and this is where the Eagles come in, was with them in 1989 when **Poco's RCA** LP *Legacy* came out and they were playing a showcase at one of our conventions in Toronto, and I was *thrilled* to meet **Randy Meisner**, former **Eagle**, and **Jim Messina** in particular.

In particular because Jim wrote in a similar NeoCountry/Rock style as the Eagles, and in between the two focal points of exposure was **Loggins & Messina** (Jim), who had a hot little number called "Your Mama Don't Dance" but it was the B-ide that got me (me, the guy that actually listened to 'B' sides; I found **Elton John's "Skyline Pigeon"** on the flipside of **"Levon"** the same way, so maybe I'm a 'B' Hive?), it was called "**Golden Ribbons**" and it stoned me, and it is to this day one of the VERY best AND VERY well-written songs, ever. Something I didn't hesitate to share with Jim, and HE was amazed anyone even heard it.

Reco- Loggins and Messina, "Golden Ribbons" YouTube

So, like **Eagles' "Last Resort,"** I was Gobsmacked while watching a **CSI:NY** in its final/closing scene, a person looking at the names on the **Vietnam War Memorial Wall** in **Washington, DC** when I hear this song come up, and I was just Holy SHIT!! *THIS* is "**Golden Ribbons**"! You mean somebody *else* knows about this treasure????

The impact of the song in this part of the show was both poignant and overwhelming as I felt myself turning into a puddle and grabbing for a bale of tissues; they NAILED it. Whew…

(TV Tunes)-.and THAT was the moment that my internet TV Tunes website idea was born; Stillborn p'raps, as it never made it off the drawing board, past an enthusiastic PowerPoint presentation I created.

I knew that this idea wasn't the Silver Bullet the Music Biz needed, but I felt it would still generate MILLIONS for Music sales Old & New, as catalogue sales would get a kick in the pants by people trying to find "**Golden Ribbons**," for example, to buy, as well as potentially being a significant breakout tool for a **NEW** Artist/Group, breaking them to consumers from Film/TV and *THEN* to Radio for more Love, the point being proven!

But, unfortunately, I didn't/don't have the technical expertise to develop this, nor did I have the money to move this ahead, still don't.

I know there are a few of these types of sites on the internet, or were, but possibly not as robust or driven or interactive as my concept; that may simply come down to Promotion/Public awareness.

I **DID** put this out there at my Raytirement party, by mentioning it in my parting shot/shout-out. But if I was pitching, nobody was catching, as the response to inviting people to call me about it had the result best described as a **Jimmy Buffet** song: **"If the phone doesn't ring, it's me."**

So, it's hard to soar with **The Eagles** when you can't get off the ground, and, by-the-way? "**Poco**" is Spanish for "a little' or 'not very much," and this has been **much** ado about a little **something.**

CHATTER #26

CHRIS REA

So, whatever happened to the guy that put out the *Whatever Happened to Benny Santini?* album, **Chris Rea**? The title track is worth the price of admission itself!

That guitar-slinging Charlie Watts doppelganger had a run of hits that also included **"Fool If You Think It's Over,"** and the FABULOUS **"Gonna Buy a Hat,"** a MUST for any impending shitstorm!

I never had the pleasure of working with him but I did have the pleasure of working his records.

SHIPWRECK (AND A TRAIN WRECK OR TWO TOO)

I have had Artist Media interviews go south for any number of reasons over the years (I don't have shoes…what?), but this one was unique.

JACKED!

jacksoul was a fine R&B group from Toronto; the voice was Haydain Neale, and it was brought to us by no less than our President, Paul Alofs, as the BIG BMG priority. They were easy to work with, particularly Haydain.

Things were going along swimmingly, as the group came to Vancouver to play Richard's on Richards and a CBCTV interview was arranged and confirmed, in advance; so much for good intentions, the same stuff the road to Hell is paved with.

We were all waiting at Richard's for the ball to roll, but it didn't; there we were and there they weren't. I made a flurry of phone calls to no avail, until I caught a call from the contact who sleepily advised they'd slept in and forgot about it, a real Brown Trouser moment for me, and No, it couldn't happen at all that day!

... aaaaand that's lunch!

I didn't order anything as I had enough egg on my face for everyone.

The Jack Came Back!

Haydain and company returned sometime later to perform at The Vogue Theater, Presented by Radio Z95, where the current single was playing and doing fine, right up to the moment the Big Z95 guy came up to me backstage and let it drop that he'd taken their song OFF the air that afternoon! WTF! I couldn't believe my ears, what kind of a JackAss does that?! Controlling an urge to kill and dismember, I asked WHY? He said that Haydain had told the Big JA that there was a new single coming (there's ALWAYS new singles coming from a new album!) so he dropped the current song without even listening to the next single (which I didn't even know of at that point) to hear if it fit the station's sound; THIS is why I wasn't allowed to carry a firearm when working.

I reluctantly mentioned this to Haydain after the show so as not to upset the performance, and he was as stunned as I was.

I was considering stopping going to the Media to support my Artists and rather going to a Medium so THEY could tell us what was going to go on, yeah.

I sent head office a Nuclear Missive on email about what transpired and awaited the shock and awe to followed the next morning from Toronto, altho it was nothing like what happened in Manhattan, as the next day was 9/11.

Straight out of bed in the morning, without having heard nor seen any media, I called Z95 to see what could be done to restore the song on their airwaves, but was blown off by the Big JA saying he couldn't talk as he was trying to get a big story on air, so later then.

I turned on the TV just in time to see he second plane fly into the Tower; shock.

It goes without saying that head office's reaction was Ballistic, evoking instant bad blood. I didn't need them to phone me; I could hear them yelling.

We had no problem with the station itself, we loved it (up to…), but it was decidedly in need of an ummmmmmm…demise.

Time wounds all heels, and JA moved on to inflict himself on another Radio Station in Ontario, which in a sense was fitting, as I'd always thought of him as an EastHole.

Haydain and Jacksoul carried on, but luck wasn't on his side as he was in a VERY bad traffic accident, nearly killing him in 2007. He survived but fell to Cancer in 2009.

Here's the web link to check out the band: https://www.jacksoul.com/

MONUMENTS GALORE:

At RCA we had a **Winnipeg** group called "**Monuments Galore**" (and THAT means????…anyone?) come to town for a couple shows, and altho they weren't "ours" per se (it was a Buy/Sell deal: Sales but no Promo), we thought we'd give them a leg up anyway. They were a bit of an odd-looking lot, like a drawer full of unmatched socks; each member looked as though they should be playing in different bands.

Part (almost all) of the Media work was an interview on **Radio CBC** with **Robert Ouimet**, but when we arrived, we were advised it was cancelled due to Robert running his boat up on a reef in the Gulf Islands and getting stranded, just like we were, as this was our **ONLY** Radio interview. The group was too new, and I felt like Raymondson Crusoe, and no, it wasn't Friday.

For the most part, as an opening act, the band was well received and quite over the top about it, which served to deepen their depression the next night when they headlined at that bastion of Counter Culture, **The Town Pump**, as the audience was conspicuous in their absence. There was, however, little they could say about it, **UNLIKE** the night **our** Vancouver Rock Group signing **The Bloody Chicletts** played **"86 Street"** as an opening act when their fey little keyboard player confronted me with a shitload of attitude, **DEMANDING** to know what kind of **Promo Man** was I, as there was nobody in the venue!!

Well…Two things; One, the doors aren't open yet and Two, don't try talking to me again like that before your 3rd successful album is out, **ASS *HOLE*.**

The **Bloody Chicletts** was a Studio project that formed as a band AFTER the record and deal was done and they thought they should cobble together an actual group from cousins and friends for live performances. They didn't do well at that, as was evident when they were brought to Toronto for a showcase in front all the arbiters of Taste.they couldn't play up to the record, it was said.

Lots of attitude, little aptitude.

Vancouver Sun's John Mackie called **Monuments Galore Monuments of Bore** and my friend, **Tom Harrison of *The Province***, thought another BMG act, **Big House**, should have been in one.

Big House were a **BMG** Priority that didn't ring Tom's bell, and that's OK, you can't like them all, tho I did try to get his support with an interview. He, however, was reluctant and therein lies a good lesson: **Do Not** paint Media into a corner, whether they are friend or friendly, or you may find yourself friendless, as it's wrong and it doesn't work. Let the chips fall where they may. Our business is built upon good relationships and they shouldn't turn bad; you may very well need them on another day for something they'd be glad to cover.

There's a fine line between Promotion and Pestering; **don't cross it.**

In this instance, we launched **Big House** at a Media/Retail showcase at "**86 Street**" on Halloween in 1991 in conjunction with **The Fox**. With the venue decked out for the evening, we had a **Slammer/Dungeon** built inside for our guests to mix and mingle with the band before they played.

That's right, ADMIT ONE, you don't get to take your date to Prison, if you have a date in Prison, they're there already…pass the soap.

It all went well until I got home and dumped a pile of **Big House** t-shirts I had gotten for give-away on the kitchen counter, at which point I was hard pressed to explain the pairs of Ladies Thongs that rolled out.

God, I hate my life.

SIX CYLINDER-

Signed them too. Good guys, Good "Chickens," but "Beyond Hope," there was nothing.

Bk Row (L) Leagh Alden, Band Member, R2, Front Seated 6 Cylinders and John Ford (3rd from R) cracking everyone up with his Chicken/Road joke, I guess. 1980. Photo by Joness Bowie

SKIN-

Handy stuff. Kind of the glue that holds us ALL together, without it we'd just fall apart, literally.

If your skin is thin, the rigors of the Music Biz are likely not for you; it's a tough business, you should have *really* thick skin, if not Bark.

SLOAN-

They always called me "**Uncle Ray**" and loved the stories. Good Guys. One day "**I Love a Long Goodbye**" will be a big Country hit.

Reco- Sloan, "I Love a Long Goodbye"

JO-EL SONNIER-

One of the **BEST** experiences I had in County and in general as well; he wanted to take YOUR picture! What a GREAT and under-rated artist.

Reco- Jo-El Sonnier, "No More One More Time," "Tear Stained Letter," "I've Slipped Her Mind," "Baby Hold On"

RED SOVINE-

For forgetting that I was his Rep during an autograph session at **Treachers Records** and calling me **"Teddy Bear,"** his hit at the time. Red was getting on in years and his appearance at the Newton Inn that night may only have been an early show. Yeah.

CHATTER #27

BRITNEY SPEARS-

We first saw her on **Howie Mandel's** afternoon talk show when **"Oops…"** was breaking and we were stunned; the sound was SO bad it was like she couldn't sing, huh.

The singing Spears I prefer personally is **Billy Jo Spears**, Country singer. It's a matter of taste really, I mean it's not Rocket Surgery right? Your Vacancy?

I'll never forget Britney's Boobie-Gate when the Media realized she seemed to suddenly be looking her breast, BEST, sorry, had to y'know. We now know her Mom bought them for her (and I didn't ask for a 12" Pianist!) but then, the official line was "a growth spurt," playing the Devil's Avocado, my question was...*her* or the Surgeons Bank Account?

Now, some bone-head booked her for a 'Residency' in Las Vegas and tix sales stink. They're calling this the **"Piece of Me"** show; maybe rethink that and call it the "Piece of Meat" show?

SPONTANEITY-

Some of the best moments of Rock & Roll come without warning; watching **Paul McCartney** on a televised concert in **Liverpool** at the (New) **Cavern Club** introduce an oldie from his previous band when some wag in the audience yells out, "**Satisfaction**!" to which Paul instantly responds..."Fook Off!" I thought I'd die laughing, I could hardly breathe.

Watching **Keith Richards** in "Hail, Hail Rock & Roll" endure an on-camera dressing down from his Headmaster, **Chuck Berry,** for playing one of his songs incorrectly, a song that Keith no doubt played HUNDREDS of times, and have Chuck walk him thru the incorrect part like a schoolboy while Keith no doubt was biting down **HARD** on his own tongue. Keith would later say that **Chuck Berry** gave him more headaches than **Mick Jagger**, but it still was a great show.

... and isn't it sad that **Chuck Berry**, one of the Founding Fathers and Prime Architects of Rock & Roll, whose music helped develop so many great artists, would suffer the indignity of having his BIGGEST Radio Hit be "**My Ding-a-ling**," a song about his dick? It's a good thing his name wasn't **Dick Berry**, or else he'd could have written "My Chuck-a-luck"?

Finally, an aural experience, as it was on vinyl (*The London Howlin' Wolf Sessions*) only as I recall, Howlin' Wolf (Chester Burnett) stopping his All-Star British band mid-song to dress down **Eric Clapton** for playing his song the wrong way! It's priceless, but it was his song, who knew better?

That's Rock & Roll, warts and all.

Reco- Howlin' Wolf, "Ain't Superstitious," *The London Howlin' Wolf Sessions*, "Little Red Rooster" dress down

RICK SPRINGFIELD-

He showed up so late for a **New Year's Eve** concert at **The Orpheum** it was almost next year, and had me prove that I could still run for my life from the Tsunami of shrieking girls rolling to the stage when he finally came on. I had to do the same several other times, including with **T.Rex** (I ran faster than **Marc Bolan's** Eyeliner!), the **Hudson Brothers**, and the **Stampeders**, to name a few.

Stage Mothers- Run, No, **RUN**...*FASTER!*

STAMPEDERS-

Ronnie, Rich and Kim.

My first Big act to go on the road with. Did a lot of work, had a lot of fun. Helped "**Sweet City Woman**" become a hit in Canada, which then went on to become a *huge* Worldwide hit.

Banjos and Bag-pipes work every time, just ask the Paul of Kintyre.

Rich had the first double guitar I'd seen (6 and 12 string). Ronnie became a "King" cuz Van Sprang didn't have that rang. Kim Berly later became Kimball Fox in "**The Cry**" which really wasn't answered, altho I LOVED their "leave your bones in the hall" thing.

Worked with **Wolfman Jack** on one of their shows; what a character and WHAT a Radio show!

They held sway in the Pop '70s with the aforementioned "**Sweet City Woman**," which set up the ones to follow, among them the sinfully fun "**Devil You**" (and HEY! How come nobody raised Hell about *that* Satanic

Message, or did they just hate **Cowboy Junkies**, hmmm?!), then there's the astute **"Then Came the White Man,"** a sentiment worthy of future Hipster **Gord Downie**.

Randy Bachman's pre-**BTO** band **Brave Belt's** name was also a throw to the Indigenous belt worn by Plains tribes and one has to include Canada's **Neil Young** as an empathizer from the 'Peg.

(*See 'There Goes the Neighborhood' by Rs truly for more on the subject of 1st Peoples www.aladinladner.simplesite.com/411210875)

On a memorable night out/off in YVR with the **Stampeders**, we went to see the early **BTO** playing at **Pharaoh's Retreat** in Gastown where they were invited onstage to jam, Randy riffing the intro to "**Wild Eyes**" by way of introduction; what a memory.

Their star rising, they had quite an impact with the kids, FM radio not having taken a foothold, or toehold, for that matter, and they weren't yet distracted by the likes of **Marilyn Manson** or **Tool**; plenty of time for that later.

They were a big draw as I recall from being with them in Victoria and later at a concert venue on West Pender Street in downtown Vancouver, Presented by Pop Powerhouse **CKLG/73** and **REAL Roy**, who asked for 100 copies of their new LP to give away to the fans, and at THAT announcement commenced a wailing tsunami wall of women charging for the records, at which point we dropped the records and *RAN*, creating our own stampede for our lives!

Reco- Stampeders, "Sweet City Woman," "Johnny Lightning," "Wild Eyes," "Hit the Road Jack" (w The Wolfman!), "Devil You," "Then Came the White Man"

Here's Real Roy (Hennessy) and Really Ray with The Stampeders (L>R) Rich, Kim, Ronnie. You may have noticed that I'm wearing Roy's Cap and trousers while he's wearing my Jacket; I'm trying to not remember how that happened. Musical Clothing?

want more????

www.stampeders.net

KENTISH STEELE-

Became one of Vancouver's prime practitioners of Soul/R&B, and when they (His Band, the Shantelles) were just starting, I recall booking them into the Sunset Community Centre for a dance.

He was a rising star, joining the R&B Galaxy of **Night Train Revue**, and **Jayson Hoover & The Epics**, among a few others. In one of John Pearson's early bands, their singer, **Al Forchuk** (had a full beard by 9 and could get served in a Liquor Store at 12, no questions asked) would leap up off the stage and do the Splits in mid-air, then drop down to the stage in full Split and spin up and out, and never missed a beat!

Kentish was a very visually impressive entertainer and I was very impressed with his "**I am the Son of God**" routine (that I caught at **Oil Can Harry's** one night) and then burst, nay! *Erupted* into a Soul celebration of "Aquarius"; riveting.

But, I think the coolest thing I ever saw was him and the **Shantelles** at **Exhibition Gardens**; most singers could dance. MAN, could they dance! **James Brown** put us ALL on our Good Foot. We used to practice before going to dances; really, spins, special footwork, and the big one, the splits, THAT was hard, but we did it.

Now, there we were at the show, and Kentish is a whirling Dervish of footwork and then I noticed a white guy in front of the stage dancing his *ass* off like Kentish. Kentish took the challenge, and what a performance between the two in the dance-off, when the white guy takes off his sport jacket in mid pirouette, drops it on the floor beside him, and then, while Kentish and God and everyone looked on, he dropped down doing the Splits, hooked a finger into the collar of his jacket and in one smooth effort, rose back up, turned on his heel with his jacket over his shoulder and walked off the floor, ending the duel with Kentish helplessly looking on. *SHUT* UP!

STEPS-

I should call this one "**Mis-Steps.**" I saw they were HUGE in England and asked for a release here in Canada; be careful what you wish for.

Opened for **Britney Spears**, a huge break here, but their Management knew nothing of the Canadian, nor I suspect the American market, and was an overbearing ASS to deal with. He blew a GREAT opportunity by not allowing Photogs to shoot them because they lacked the credentials he hadn't issued himself, then blamed ME, Pardon, that's YOUR job mate

People like this should wear Steel-toed footwear cuz when you shoot yourself in the foot, you don't lose any toes. Watch that first "Step"

CAT STEVENS-

Steven Georgiou.

The "Cat" has had nearly as many career starts as a Cat has lives, or, **Kenny Rogers**, Fried Chicken notwithstanding.

I never met nor worked with Cat, as he was distributed by TPC, but he was on **A&M Records**, an incredible little boutique label that had their own Promotion Reps. The Reps around this period were either **Liam Mullen** or **Bruce Bissell**; I'm sure they have Cat tales of their own, and both were highly capable Music Men.

Having said that, Cat was actually signed to another (Parent) label, **Chris Blackwell's Island Records** (**UK**), and both A&M/Island had incredible foresight and taste in signing artists and dedication to long-term development.

Back then when Artist development was paramount, you had 3 LPs or 3 Years; now you have 3 months or maybe 3 hours (C'mon, C'mon, C'mon! We don't have all minute!)

I haven't heard Cat's music in quite some time, but going thru my vinyl LP collection the other day, I was transferring (almost all) of the *Teaser & the Firecat* LP to my CPU, getting a second chance to hear this great & timeless music. I also found it to be quite "tropical," so it's fitting Cat's home was "**Island**."

He reminded me of **Harry Belafonte** for a new generation; see the upcoming "**Under the Influences**" chapter.

I note that he also did the painting that is the cover art for the album, and if you look at the photo on the inside of the (then) gatefold jacket and back at the painting, you might find an uncanny resemblance between Cat and the "Teaser".

He has since eschewed his Pop Music life and career and become a devout Muslim, **Yusef Islam** by name, and you can't make a "Cat" out of that, no matter how you skin it.

Michelle Stewart- Engaging. A First-Class lady, co-worker and friend, I miss her.

Here's R2 and Michelle Ma-belle; I hope Sony realized what a Special talent and person they have on their side. Michelle is smiling because she's wearing a toned down and less combustible top than I am, Old Smokey the Beer.
Shooter- Dee Lippingwell

CHATTER #28

Sir Monty Rock III- He was one of the most bizarre people I ever beheld.

The first time I laid eyes on him was when he appeared on **Johnny Carson,** and Johnny and **Ed McMahon,** the man that personified the word "Guffaw," introduced him. On comes this nattily dressed dude, jacket, bell-bottom pants, with hair down to his ass, and he performed an out-of-this world, as in "unearthly," version of **"Tennessee Waltz,"** then jumped up and started dancing like a chicken, his gangly legs akimbo, chicken scratching, and his arms bent at the waist, flapping away with his head bobbing and pecking and his mane flailing away like a cloud of angry gnats and he was SERIOUS!

His look was later upstaged by **Tiny Tim,** which gives you a visual image. **Bruce Bissell** worked with Tim and he's got stories!

Years later, **Sir Monty** is back, on one of our labels...of course (sigh); God I Hate my life.

This time he's in the persona of **Disco Tex, And His Sex-o-lettes,** which wasn't only the NAME of the act but ALL of the lyrics to their hit song of the SAME name. It was a BIG hit and should have served to alert us all to the fact that A.D.D. had set in on a large scale.

So, with this hit in hand, and hand in glove, Sir Monty and his freak show arrived to play **The Cave** here in Vancouver; you felt like a Voyeur just being around these people; So, Monty, your next gig is in Gomorrah?

SKIFFLE-

...is American slang for "rent party" where people played home-made or acoustic instruments in the kitchen for a small donation to raise enuff money to STAY in the kitchen. This was in the 1920's and largely among the Black population.

About 30 years later, "**Skiffle**" rose to prominence, largely in **England**, and largely again by **Lonnie Donegan**. It was an alternative to Big Band Pop Music of the time, which could not be easily reproduced around a kitchen table, whereas Skiffle, a blend of different elements, a Roots music and kind of contemporary of American Rock-a-Billy, could be easily played on an acoustic guitar, washboard, tea-chest bass, a harmonica, and what have you.

Lonnie Donegan was the "**King of Skiffle**" and recorded a string of hits ("**My Old Man's a Dustman**," "**Does Your Chewing Gum Lose its Flavour (On the Bedpost Overnight?)**," and more). He saw a resurgent interest in himself/Skiffle in the late 1970s with his *Puttin' On The Style* LP that featured a backing galaxy of British Rockers as a tribute to his contribution to *their* careers. It is a terrific record, a **"Must Hear"** in my humble opinion.

Reco- Lonnie Donegan, "Nobody's Child," "Puttin' On The Style"

Perhaps another analogy for Skiffle in North America in years following might have been the mutual career rise of **Led Zeppelin** and **Creedence Clearwater Revival**; both made great records, but you couldn't reproduce Zep around a kitchen table as you could CCR on a flat top guitar.

Skiffle also gave rise to another Musician of some notes, **John Lennon**, who's first band, **The Quarrymen**, played skiffle and beat a path to other Music forms and who went on to a modicum of fame, so don't say 'Piffle' to 'Skiffle'!

STONEBOLT-

Signed them, too, after their US deal went (further) South all because of my relationship w their Manager **John Iuele** (George Gosling was his partner in the bands management) from **Boston's Bottom** in Penticton. **David Wills** and I are friends to this day.

Here we all are at Cypress Bowl in 1980. Myself in the background, the Late Leigh Alden (with stiff neck) on the right, Our Masters Voice front & center, signing **Stonebolt** to **RCA**. I don't think they did posed signing shots like this before Mr ShowBiz Pants (Rs truly) showed up, but it was my idea to picture them at the 'Top of the Rock Pile' as it were.

No Photo credit so maybe it was Jimmy Hoffa, at least we now know where he is.

STONE ROSES-

We called them the Stone Noses (no reason), a work project that worked out; scored a #1 for **"Fools Gold"** on **1040 Rocks**, didn't happen **anywhere** else.

STONES-

Never met them but was a **BIG** fan from the moment I laid eyes and ears on them.

I did do something of a favor for Keith late last year, but haven't heard anything back. He may not care or maybe it wasn't such a favor. The Keef goes on.

I'd seen them on TV, but going to a theatre and seeing them on the big screen in the **T.A.M.I.** show was a first for me; I'd never experienced a Rock & Roll riot before, but the SECOND they came on, the theatre ERUPTED, people were going crazy, REALLY crazy, they were tearing the theatre apart. The Management stopped the film, put up the lights and threatened to call the Police if one more outburst happened, and it did and they didn't, but THAT was NUTS!

They've been known to nick a lick if not an entire song, so I nicked Mick when we opened our Deli in Steveston; I wrote the slogan "**It's only Crock & Rolls,** but you'll *LIKE* it!," and I did.

This is a pen & ink sketch I did of Mick a lifetime ago, one of many.

DONNA SUMMER-

I came across something interesting while going thru my vinyl LP collection and transferring them to my CPU: the **Donna Summers** *Love to Love You Baby* LP.

Interesting because there was a time when Disco was on the 12" singles we issued for DJs and Clubs to play to bump sales on the actual LP, the same as we did with 7" singles for Radio, except the 12" were limited so as not to cannibalize LP sales.

Side 1 of the LP is her 16 minute+ erotic opus, a Paean to aural sex (when I first heard this I really didn't know where to look, it was like being in someone's bedroom) and that's the entire side, much, if not exactly what the 12" single would have been. Side 2 of the LP is 5 tracks; so, is this a full LP, or is it a 12" with 5 B sides?

This was before people started to complain about there being "only one good song on an LP."

THE SUNSET BOMBERS-

When I arrived at **RCA**, they had taken on distribution of **Ariola America**, a subsidiary of the European label owned by **Bertelsmann AG**, one of the world's biggest Media companies, and it was a very successful label over there.

Due to the fact that they were in the same time zone as us, in addition to being the **RCA Promo Rep**, I was the defacto **Product Manager for Ariola** in Canada, as well, and as such would visit their LA office every couple of months, along with our RCA office there.

The head of **Ariola America** was **Jay Lasker**, formerly of **ABC/Dunhill**, and famous for his ritual of playing you a song then banging on his desk hard and loud enough to impact the Richter Scale while declaring **"it's a F**king SMASH!"** in his finest stentorian bellow.

One act he presented to us was a pseudo-Punk/Rock band called the **Sunset Bombers**. Watching the video, I commented the singer looked a little Cuckoo's nest, and he was beside himself telling us that whenever the band had a gig, they had to sign him out of a Mental Hospital, so the singer had "crazy" working for him.

I worked with them when they played Vancouver's then "**IN**" club, the **Body Shop** (a converted...guess what), run by **Bob Shure** (who later ran the Rockin' Newton Inn until it became SaveOn Foods) and the place where all the big acts played, including a fledgling **BTO**.

The night they played there, **Bob Marley** & his moving Jamaican Carnival were staying in the hotel next door, cooking their own food, using their own blend of Spices and Herbs; if the Colonel only knew!

In spite of a good launch, the Bombers bombed, but **Ariola** had some success, notably with **Ami Stewart's** "**Knock on Wood**" and a few other Disco/Dance hits. In the US, they also had Vancouver's **Prism**, but they were never able to duplicate their European successes; however, good things come to those that wait!

Jay Lasker went on to head **Motown** (before succumbing to Cancer in 1989); **GE** bought the **RCA** company in 1983, then sold off the Music division as fast as it could (I guess weird, creative people, unburdened by suit & tie and Corporate Kool-Aid didn't 'suit' them) to...wait for it! Waaaaaaait! **ARIOLA** aka BMG in Germany, proving once and for all that the tail *CAN* wag the dog!

Reco- The Sunset Bombers- "I Can't Control Myself"

CHATTER #29

THE THOMPSON TWINS-

Weren't; not *real* twins, they were a trio named after a British cartoon series, and they WERE a bit toonish (and tune-ish) looking, with their sticky-uppy hair (Tom and Alannah), except for Joe Leeway, the Dreaded one, and with their fashionably toonish clothes that had buttons the size of Man Hole covers!

Alannah was the femme fatale formerly with a heroine habit, Tom was the school teacher we all wanted, and Jo...Joe was the Black guy in charge of wearing Dreadlocks, I guess.

Watching their equally fashionable fans go around the Coliseum concourse was a bit like watching the rinse cycle of a load of Very LOUD clothes go round, a study in contrast from the Good Glam Goth a'mighty experience of **Mötley Crüe** the next night.

Here we are backstage at the Pacific Coliseum in 1985. The Thompson Twins L>R2 the Dreaded Joe Leeway. 3 contest winners, Alannah with either a crème pie or perhaps a Cumulo Nimbus cloud on her head, 2 more contest winners, Tom, winner and the aforementioned...R2. Photog- Joness Bowie

THOR-

John Mikl started out as **Mikl Body Rock** at Wrestling matches in between body slams. When I joined RCA, his was the first Rock project I got to promote. I had the feeling my 2 years promoting **KISS** successfully had something to do with my hiring; it was the same VISUAL type of thing.

Promoting a Hard Rock Mikl Metal act took some people aback as RCA was known as a **BIG** Country label (as well as the home of Elvis) and I had massive success with **Quality** with Baldemar Huerta (**Freddy Fender**), who had spent time in the joint for having one, as well as The Happiest Girl in the WHOLE USA, Biker Girl/School Teacher **Donna Fargo**. However, as I'd had previous experience and success promoting both, I handled it.

JUSTIN TIMBERLAKE-

A fine fellow whether with **NSYNC** or on his own. He went out of his way to be helpful. One time while he toured with **Christina Aguilera** (post-media Shitstorm), their **Vancouver** date had to be canceled at the last minute, as it seemed that somebody forgot to tell ALL the truck drivers they couldn't have a record other than phonograph. One couldn't cross the border and HIS truck had all the connecting thingies (it's called TOURING people, it's not new, pay attention!), so their sold-out show got blown out of the water.

While both artists were in town, only Justin's people bothered to call me to see how best to handle the Radio, Media, Fans, so they did care.

While all this was going on Christina's people had the promoter sweeping the venue with Bomb Dogs! Huh, I didn't think she was THAT bad.

R2 and JT

TOOL-

Another 5-year band. Very dark project, but when they broke...**Lyle Chausse** was huge in helping break this, kind of an inside job. Vocalist Maynard was an odd duck; when I saw them perform at the PNE Forum, I saw a small man come onstage in boxer shorts painted blue. He autographed things by pressing 5 blue fingers onto them; unique.

Sean Cordner, our **BMG Street rep** at the time, and I went to meet them the afternoon of the show, and it was weird; we went in and introduce ourselves and they kept their heads down over their bowls and continued to slurp soup; they didn't even burp at us! Walking around the venue inside I noticed a number of needles lying around and THAT always creeps me out, so needles to say, we left.

While the band was together, the audience was quickly falling apart, literally.

Some of them were so messed up on whatever, they were actually falling over, some into steel waste barrels. I think I picked up enough teeth to make a necklace.

I think the only other time I saw an audience in that shape was at a Rap show where the band, **Urban Dance Squad** (from Holland), was letting people up on stage to dive off into the crowd and surf away when one kid, a rather robust kid, like a fridge with a head, got up and dived into the crowd, which parted like Moses and the Red Sea, splitting his head open on the cement floor and then getting him rushed to Emergency to be reassembled.

Wow, an evening out, cold; Hmmm, money well spent?

TORONTO~

I can't even *count* the number of times I've been there, and each time has been an exhausting Spin-dizzy marathon. Each time, at each meeting/convention it seemed *every* meal (including Breakfast if you count eggs) was **Chicken**, top of the menu. This likely accounts for it being near the top of Ontario's Endangered Species List (Harlan Saunders would be a close 2nd). My favorite view of Toronto is from a Westbound Airplane with me giving a Float Wave.

THE TPC CREW (TAYLOR, PEARSON & CARSON/QUALITY, A&M, UA, MOTOWN, MUSHROOM)-

Gary Ritz, Calvin Lew, Wayne Bailey, Bev Shannon, and a few others. Reg (Ayres) gave us all our breaks, but we made **ourselves** successful. Great people one and all. I've lost track of **Gary Ritz** but I'd love to re-connect with him if anyone knows his whereabouts.

Here's **Calvin Lew** *and R's truly waaaaay back when we was fab, smiling and laughing at my hair & pants in our office at 1036 Richards St which would become more famously known as* "**Richards on Richards**" *in the future.*

THE TRACTORS-

Often thought to be **Ronnie Dunn's** ("**Brooks & Dunn**") former band from Oklahoma, but turns out their common ground *was* Oklahoma and both hellishly talented. Our local Country Station was possibly the **ONLY** one in North America to **NOT** play "**Baby Likes to Rock it**" when it was a **SIZZLING** hit. Later, they told me I was right and played it. I LOVE a good fight but a *timely* win is better than just being right.

Reco- The Tractors, "Baby Likes to Rock It"

They followed this up with one of the **BEST** Xmas records *ever* featuring "**Santa Claus is Coming** (In a Boogie-Woogie Choo-Choo Train)," aka "**Santa Likes to Rock It.**" They stopped short of an Easter release of "**Bunny likes to hop it**"...sigh.

Reco- The Tractors, "Santa Claus is Coming (In a Boogie-Woogie Choo-Choo Train)," "The Santa Claus Boogie"

TRAFFIC

Notably included **Dave Mason**, who had a solo career and a big hit with "**Feelin' Alright**," which was covered by **Joe Cocker**. The band also had **Jim Capaldi**, and the White Stevie Wonder, **Steve Winwood**, ambience driver.

I got my first jolt of **Steve Winwood** when I heard "**Gimme Some Lovin**" by the **Spencer Davis Group**, who were on the **Island** label; he was **Stevie Wonder/Little Richard** combined, only paler.

Then came the Traffic Jam of "**Dear Mr. Fantasy**" and a succession of brilliant albums.

My friend and (then) workmate **Calvin Lew** turned me on to **Traffic's** expansive sound with "***Shootout in the Fantasy Factory***" AND Southern Comfort, my ever since favorite drink, all in one night and I stick by all three!

Jim Capaldi was **Traffic's** drummer and I *swear* he was BORN on a back-beat!

He did a couple of solo albums, very tasty, that produced **"I've Got So Much Lovin,"** **"Low Rider,"** aaaand a true Classic, a version of **"Oh, How We Danced! (The Anniversary Song),"** written by none other than the little tramp himself, **Charlie Chaplin**!

Those White English boys sure got Soul!

TRAGICALLY HIP-

We, at **RCA**, STARTED these guys off, another label made all the money…how many times???? Quite a project!

Good guys, good band, unassuming lot. Gord & I expounded on one of our favorite books, **Dee Brown's "Bury My Heart at Wounded Knee,"** as we shared an empathy for the Indigenous amongst us, something Gord *always* hung on to.

*Things you wish you NEVER said Dept:

While trying to get (then) **CKLG-FM** to go another track deeper into the EP and being told by the **MD** "I think we're done with the **Tragically Hip**" the station's (**The FOX**) future House Band!

Reco- The Tragically Hip, "Small Town Bringdown" 1987 **RCA**

The first song off the **Tragically Hip's** first self-titled EP album release from 1987.

Photo courtesy of Kevin Shea

A BRILLIANT band that stood its ground *and* the test of time and made an indelible mark in Music history. You see, it pays to colour *outside* the lines!

Their first Canadian (club) tour was mayhem, with people throwing things (and Gord throwing back), being kicked out of clubs and more bcuz the club people were used to cover bands or hard rockers and these guys were too Hip for the rooms, but that would all change.

They made a lot of good music, the least of which was pretty damn good. I am presently quite taken with the brilliant "**Grace, Too**"; hope you are as well.

CHATTER #30

TREACHERS-

Original owner, **Neville** (Go Naked!) **Treacher**; Music Man and Professional Nudist. Sold it to **Richard Watt**, and there began the Glory Days at ("Vancouver's Home of Country Music") and the Back Room Bar.

Neville was a shrewd businessman that donated singles to my High School's (John Oliver) Radio Club that broadcast (closed circuit) at Noon hour all the hits in exchange for plugs for his store.

For a Music fan on a budget, his 59 cent singles bin was a Treasure Trove and was where I found my first **Rolling Stones** record...and speaking of them, here's some irony: I was browsing in the store when a **London Records** (where the 5 louts had been signed) Label Sales Rep came in all dressed up in a suit and tie, trying to promote the **Rolling Stones** first LP to Neville, the Irony being that the Stones would be fit to be tied rather than wear one.

What a fun crew! Deep-World's biggest Elvis fan (Elvis Maharesley), Sally, Linda (Two Beers), Gary Borsato- the Human Parrot (Awk! Whatcha got for free! (whistle), Hardy and his sister "Laurel" (what a team!), the FUN we had.

And who could forget the Saturday morning visits from "**The Bowling Team**" who would arrive in a gaggle, re-arrange the stock unalphabetically, Pee on the floor, then "split" for 'Fraser Lanes' to throw Bowling Balls at each other. Good times.

Awarding the **CKWX SuperCountry Honky Tonkin'**
*contest winner @ Treachers Back in the day
(L>R) Richard Watt- Owner of Treachers, Red Robinson- then CKWX Morning
Man among Morning Men, The Winner! and R's truly under my hatbrella*

I wanted to do a print layout ad with *attitude*, but was told, in no uncertain terms, that I could **NOT** use alcohol to sell product, so I did it anyway. This ran in the Georgia Straight 1978, so...don't tell ME what I can't do, cuz I'll DO it!

TREBLE CHARGER-

Hey! HERE'S a ROYAL flash!

There was a time when there were two Rock/FM Radio Stations in **YVR** (**Xfm** and **The Fox**), a Promo Rep's terminal Migraine, as both tried to one-up the other continually and Record Reps were the meat in a Slam Sandwich. So, this is a Promo Rep's Nightmare, and I should mention here that Promo Reps don't dream, they *have* Nightmares, they've just been having them so long they *THINK* it's dreaming.

We had **Treble Charger** coming in for a show, and **Xfm** got the "Presents," and courtesy requires the "Presenting" station get 1st dibs on interviews and activities, but NOT to the exclusion of other Radio/Media.

The MD of **Xfm** asked me for an interview and to have them play guitars during that, BUT stressed he did NOT want them playing in their **Fox** interview, OK.

So the next week I'm at **The Fox** for my weekly meeting with their MD, and guess who's sitting in the **Fox MD chair**? The MD from Xfm jumped ship!

Now this same guy says to me that he wants **Treble Charger** to PLAY during their interview! I paused (for effect) and looking him straight in the eye said that I couldn't as I had promised the other station (**Xfm**) that I wouldn't and that I was a man of my word *and* that I KNEW he got that. No more was said; Check, Mate.

Having said that, when **Xfm** found out what time the **Trebs/Fox** interview was, they did everything in their Frequency Modulated power, short of announcing a Bomb scare, to distract listeners from tuning in; so, how old are these people? I swear to God (or insert your Deity here) that I would wake up with a full head of Black hair and by the time I got home it was White and thin, daily.

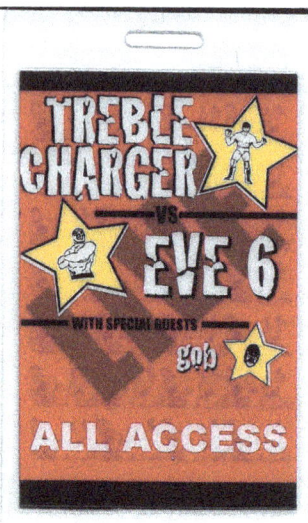

I have known a LOT of people in Radio during my tenure and I've watched some of them come from AssBucket BC to do some great things, and they have all my respect, but there were a few people in Broadcasting that shouldn't be operating a Toaster, never mind a Radio Station.

Stay tuned.

Promo Monkey: My Life as a BellHop in the Waldorf Hysteria

2002 saw Treble Charger get Gold (50,000 units sold) for **Wide Awake Bored**, *presented to them in front of their live audience at the Starfish Room in Vancouver. Pretty intoxicating stuff for both band and fans! Here is the backstage pic with the BMG Posse, the band is thrilled, and Rosie, sitting on my knee, got Gold and a Goose it seems, so Golden Goose?*

Here we are presenting the people that made The Fox ROCK with "Gold" for Treble Charger (L>R)- Rob Robson-one of the nicest people you could hope to meet in the Radio/Music Biz who pulled his hair out weekly just listening to me wheedle and whine, Bob Mills-Mr. PD Fox who's wearing Robbie's hair for a hat, the Wonderful May Lam, the Uber-Capable Terry McBride who made Nettwerk work, R's truly in prison denims, and BMG Toronto's Dave Harris who was there to make sure they actually GOT the award and that I didn't melt them down for myself; like HE never thought of that!

Reco- Treble Charger, "American Psycho," "Red"

Trooper-

My one association was the **RCA** LP. Great guys, I remember them from **Applejack**, and that's a LONG time ago. Great bunch o' guys.

Here's my all-time favorite Trooper tune...**Janine** www.youtube.com/watch?v=nxzBNOzu6hc

Courtesy of Ra McGuire

CHATTER #31

T.REX-

Marc Bolan used to tell people he lived with a Wizard; Really? Pull the other one!

He was the first Rock Star I saw wearing Make-up and Mascara off-stage. What a goof. **Mickey Finn** was alright, but Marc? If you have to pay people to be your friend, something's screwy; Bang a Wrong.

I first met his Bass player **Jack Green** there, who would become something of a Solo priority for **RCA**.

When I hooked up with **T.Rex**, it was the downside of their career, but they were still hugely popular. In Victoria, we were all scared the fans would crush the limo from sheer weight on it trying to get on *and* IN it.

I kept away from the Nasal spray bottle being passed around the Dressing Room and was amazed to see, after the show, Marc shove all food left over in the dressing room into a canvas mail bag to be taken back to the hotel; I thought, aren't you rich? Maybe that's how he stayed that way.

In Vancouver, Marc threatened to break **Vaughn Palmer's** (**Vancouver Sun**) nose if he called him a Punk one more time during a Press conference. I was also shocked to discover that his Road Manager couldn't read, *couldn't read English,* and he **WAS**!

Backstage at the concert, things turned into a real "Gong" show, as Marc, wanting a certain recreational refreshment and wasn't getting any, so he threw a Five foot nothing **FIT** and was *leaving* until somebody got him, um, the real thing? The show went on, but the headlines in the next day's papers said it all: "**T. Wrecks!**" How the mighty have fallen, bang a dong… heavy sigh.

TUESDAY-

As a weekday was originally named after Tyr, a God of the Nordic people (Tyr's-day), and the Greeks named it after Ares, their God of War, and while this entry isn't about warfare, it is about making some noise. *THIS* **Tuesday** was a Canadian Record label helmed by **Greg Hambleton** and distributed by **Quality/TPC** here in BC. Greg's brother Fergus was also a recording artist, but not with us so he's not a player in this story.

The Ontario group **Steel River** was **Tuesday's** first signing, and they scored with "**Ten Pound Note**" from their first LP, their biggest impact at Top 40 Radio. This was followed by "**Southbound Train**" from their sophomore album, which to me was a better record, but "Ten Pound Note" remains their signature track.

I've just been listening to their albums as I go thru them to transfer from Vinyl to my CPU, and I find quite a bit of their stuff stands the test of time. In fact, considering that in 1970 FM Rock Radio was almost non-existent, they were probably ahead of their time, and might have been bigger with that outlet.

Tuesday Records provided some important links for my future to me. It connected me to some pretty key players locally, as it was thru them that I met **Bruce Allen**. We were both at **Vancouver Int'l Airport** to meet Greg, as Bruce had flown him in to produce his (then) big act "**Crosstown Bus**," a single called "**Josie**" I believe, that got some play at least locally, on then-Top 40 Powerhouse **CKLG-AM**, home of "**Real**" Roy Hennessy, centerfold to Women of Vancouver and beyond.

I believe I saw **Crosstown Bus** play **The Commodore**. The Singer/Guitarist was wearing powder blue bib overalls, I think.

Bruce never did take the "Bus" after all, but wound up in a Silver Vet with Gold Wheels and plate that said "**Unruly**"; he is truly "driven."

Enter **Shelly Siegel**, who had yet to Mushroom, but was booking some shows, one of which was at the **Cloverdale (Rodeo) Fairgrounds** headlining our own **Steel River**, an adversarial bunch if ever I met one. Maybe they had played Ontario Place and "made it" by then?

They were highly opinionated arguers that went out of their way to discourage local Retail support, notably by pissing off the buyer, **Leigh Bordignon** from **A&B Sound**, at a Meet & Greet reception we had arranged for them; please stop helping.

Seems they flew in on Wing & A Prayer Airways, as all they had was a gig and a hotel room, plus a Manager who it was said would later disband the band after giving away, to curry favor with various individuals, percentages of them exceeding 100%, thereby earning the "Shareholders" a robust 4/5 of fuck all, metrically or Imperially.

While I was working at TPC/Quality, I was also playing in the band "**BigFoot**" that friend **Jerome Walliser** and I put together, and while I was Steel River's Driver, he was their Roadie, driving their rented equipment to the gig. It wasn't overly well attended if memory serves, sending Steel River into a snit. They were not being shy of letting everybody know their bias for Toronto, something that ALWAYS goes over big out here in the West, uh huh, prior to ending their set and smashing their rented equipment; that'll show us!

So Shelley took a bit of a bath with **Steel River**, but would recover over time with a lot of **Heart**.

I'm pretty sure **Tuesday Records** opened on a Monday and closed on a Friday, just not in the same week; Da Do Ron-Ron-Ron, Da Do Ron-Ron.

CHATTER #32

TUNE TOONS-

I have a passion for scribbling and a penchant for scrawling.

I've been drawing ever since I was old enough to eat a crayon (Mmm... Yellow!).

My big break as an Artist came one day at **TPC/Quality** when I was still the warehouse guy, doodling away while I listened to **"Hair"** by **The Cowsills** (which included Billy!) until it was all right there in front of me! Reg Ayres, the Branch Manager, saw it and sent it to Quality in Toronto, where they turned it into a Poster/hand-out for Retailers to further draw attention to the single. I was over the Moon.

Hundreds of Hand-Drafts later, I created the Poster for one of my favorite bands, **CCR**, a high-point at the time and a career milestone for me later. It was my first time creating Caricatures of REAL people instead of just making 'toons. I was taken back stage at one of their local shows, The **Agrodome** I think, where they sighed and signed it; what a break for me!

In High School, I majored in English and Art, BUT, ever the willful student, I was going to do Art MY way; don't mark me for what I can't do, mark me for what I CAN. In Grade 12, one Art project produced two collages based on Pop Music at that time, and were so well received, they went on display in the school Trophy Case. I had NO idea then that I was creating Pop Art. I still have them today, hanging framed in my office; Time Capsules.

In my Portfolio (Sounds like a disease...EW! *YOU* have PORTFOLIO! You should SEE somebody 'bout that!), there are PILES of Artwork. One of my favorite 'toons is a Cornucopia collective of 60's Pop Culture: Music, Books, Movies-Horror, Sci-Fi, Tarzan, and all dressed accordingly. I think I called it "Swap Meat," as everyone was trading something, and I LOVE a play on words.

I never made a penny with a pencil (and thanks to Stephen Harpers latest foray into Finance, now I never will), but the enjoyment is, priceless.

TYMPANI FOR THE DEAFLE-

The Tympanic Membrane is your Eardrum.

A Tympanist is a drummer.

To be Tympanicly challenged is to be deaf.

All this is because I am reminded, by her then appearance in Vancouver, of **Dame Evelyn Glennie**, who I once worked with as she was on **RCA's Classical** Roster, and she was appearing here with the VSO.

I met and picked her up at YVR, and drove her to her hotel, all the while chattering away like a Magpie, but I found only part of what I was saying was getting thru, the reason being that she was deaf; it would have been helpful to know that in advance.

Face to face we was fine, as she could read my lips, but the moment one of us turned away...

I opened this by talking about Eardrums, here's why: Dame Evelyn was a percussionist, a drummer, and deaf. When I played drums, some people thought that I was deaf, and I darned near was because that was before monitors, so we couldn't really hear what we were playing and it all just got louder and louder.

Dame Evelyn, on the other hand, had an inherited condition; she wasn't hard on the eyes, just hard on her ears, BUT, say what you will, she made the best of it so I guess there's just nothin' like a 'Dame'!

CHATTER #33

This week we find me under a variety of influences including Calypso, "Race" Records, Rock & Roll, and go from the Musical to the Muse-icle and a record that never should have made it to air, but did.

The Japanese have Haiku, which is a 3 line poem of 17 syllables; mine are more like a Hai*CHOO*! (Bless you!), which are composed of a number of Limes, salt, a shot and several silly-bles.

UNDER THE INFLUENCE-

The first music I can remember hearing was from **Harry Belafonte**.

Living with my Uncle & Aunt in Frog Hollow, Burnaby, my cousin Wendy and I were given a tin wind-up phonograph player that played these 45s. The selection was all Classics today: "**Marianne**," "**Jamaica Farewell**," "**Mama Look A Boo-Boo (Day)**," and the "**Banana Boat Song (Day-O!)**," among others. It was 'Calypso' but we didn't know that, but we LOVED it!

Harry was Black, and we didn't know/didn't care about that either, and we LOVED him! Still do; our ears were colour blind, it was all a great big happy noise to us.

Years later, with **RCA**, the Movie *Beetlejuice* came out and was an instant hit. I recall the scene with the Football team on the stairs singing "**Day-O!**" and it was very effective. Next day at the office, I ordered some copies of Harry's Hits and sent them to key Radio Stations to get play on that track; the silence was deafening. Nobody wanted to "play"; if YOU do then that'll make two of us.

Reco- Harry Belafonte, "Banana Boat Song (Day-O!)" Original *Beetlejuice* Soundtrack

...but I digress (Hm, do you think I suffer from Indigression?)

In my early teens, I was Gobsmacked by some guy calling himself "**Little Richard**"; he must have been kidding, as the sound and energy that came off that **45 (*Good Golly, Miss Molly*)** was **MASSIVE**, and that single singular jolt of (e=mc2) changed EVERYTHING for me.

Leon Russell, the Master of Space & Time, dubbed him "the undiluted Queen of Rock & Roll" in his Paean to Richard, "**Crystal Closet Queen**," which is a Fireball of energy itself. But back then I knew nothing of Colour, I just LOVED the noise, it was some strong, magical shit!

Reco- Leon Russell, "Crystal Closet Queen"

When all this Rock & Roll was coming out, however, especially music by Black artists it was widely shat upon by people too old and tired to dance. Records like **Little Richard's** and **Chuck Berry's** (for example) were called **Race Records** in the Music Business/Radio, and some whites were supremely against white kids hearing these, fearing that it would corrupt us!...Hey! ***THERE*** you are! What kept ya? I got my hand basket, let's go **Rock & Roll!**

This attitude got worse the further South you went. One might get the impression that with some Ring-ass Rednecks, the only thing they hated more than racialized people was the hard work they saved them from.

It is to **RCA Nashville's** eternal credits that, once having signed the brilliant **Charley Pride**, him being Black and singing Country, that they worked his early records at Radio while successfully keeping ANY photos of him out of sight!

For more on that, see my adventures with Charley in "**Country 42.**"

There are a few people in the Public Eye outside of the Music circle that I admire as Great Individuals, people like **Abraham Lincoln** (who died in vain), **JFK, Dr. King, President Obama** (for being first, twice), as well as **Emiliano Zapata**, and **Pancho Villa** (to a lesser degree), the latter of whom both also died in vain. Sometimes it seems losing causes are the only ones worth fighting for.

In Canada, if **Mike Holmes** ran for **PM**, I'd vote for him in a minute; he seems a genuinely Good man that inspires confidence, which is more than I can say about the incumbent Pillsbury Dough Boy and a lot of others.

One of Canada's finest writers, to me, is the late **Stuart McLean**. I fell over him, actually, when somebody lent me a book of his and I haven't put him down since.

John Steinbeck is my favorite writer in the WORLD, hands down; his stuff has a humble salt-of-the-earth humility to it, pick anything. Also, **Larry McMurtry** (*Lonesome Dove*, I must have read that 6 times!) has a similar quality, as does **James Michener** (*Centennial, Texas*), **Dee Brown** (I've read ***Bury My Heart at Wounded Knee*** at least as many times as *Lonesome Dove*) and **Mitch Albom** (*The Five People You Meet in Heaven*); if THAT doesn't move you, you're already dead. **Twain/Clemens, Winston Groom**, who wrote *Forrest Gump*, one of the finest reads I've ever had, and, of course, my first Author, **A.A. Milne**; if you haven't read him then "Pooh" on you, get cracking, he's one for the Ages, ALL of them.

VANGELIS-

broke "**Spiral**" on **CKLG-FM**, one of the first **A3** tracks, shudn't have happened, but it did. Their then MD, **Dave Chesney** did that.

Reco- Vangelis, "Spiral"

CHATTER #34

Icing the rhyme...

VANILLA ICE-

Aka **Robert Van Winkle,** known to me as Dip Van Winkle. So, your Chilliness, do you ever create anything that isn't a cut/paste of someone else's inspiration? I call that comment "icing the punk".

Then there was "**Snap!**", a former U.S. G.I. looked like a *slightly* smaller version of Shaq, based in Germany, got a label deal, came to North America on tour burning bridges all the way, was violently abusive towards Gays; the lineup for Lawsuits starts over here! Get fitted early!

He came to Vancouver, played a sold-out All-Ages show at **The Commodore,** swore at the audience, and stormed off after about 20 minutes then wisely came back.

A real charmer to deal with. Beat up his Road Manager in the Van after the gig then broke his leg for good measure; NOT the showbiz expression!

Finally "**Snap!**" snapped as there were SO many lawsuits, there was nowhere left to tour without a suer. The MC's name was Turbo B, I'm guessing the "B" stands for Butt-Head?

Puff Daddy followed this class act (3rd), real name **Sean Combs**. He was so full of himself, if he fell off his Ego he'd be killed on impact. He was a college boy Rap Poseur and his street cred was a REAL G, the **Notorious B.I.G.** aka

Christopher Wallace, a name not as imposing as his Rap name, and he was also so big he had his own Zip Code.

My greatest fear (of him) was that he might fall on me.

He was also a bonafide violent Crack dealer and his turf was wherever he was standing at the time. It should also be said that he was a victim of his environment.

"**Biggie**" also died in a hail of gunfire while being driven to an Industry event (Music, not Dope, but Def) during a dispute with (or should I say, at the END of ?) **Tupac Shakur**, possibly over the spelling of his name, so I guess maybe Tupac got the last word...yo.

Puffy was unharmed in another vehicle and went into hiding, possibly because it made it look like someone was after him too. Later, in an attempt to throw off his imagined pursuers, he changed his name to **P. Diddy**, possibly because "**P. Idiot**" was already taken by some otha foo'.

Puff brought his not inconsiderable stable of stars to Vancouver (where he made them bow to him on stage, just to show his pee-pees...Sorry! PEEPS! who had the biggest dick, or in his case who WAS the biggest dick!) for a concert, just before Christmas one year. By dint of good timing, I was on holiday and didn't have to deal with this over-bearing cock-knocker, but the poor people that **DID** deal with him & his crew were getting whiplash from his meteor shower of last minute, U-Turn-on-a-dime, flash cut Media changes. I'm wondering if the "P doesn't stand for "Princess"?

This just in: **Piddy Diddy**, or whoever he fancies himself to be today (Tuesdiddy?), is testing his own (heavy sigh) TV brand "**Revolt TV**" and I'm sure it will be all of that.

This shud prove a quantum leap for his Narcissism, but he makes a point by having this brand compatible with social media, so he'll be able to reach that key demographic and get his not inconsiderable ego stroked that way too. Maybe he can set it up so he has his own show about preening and posing opposite **Arsenio Hall** so the public will have to choose which "Arse" they want to subject themselves to.

CHATTER #35

WAYLON & WILLIE-

Played the Coliseum here one year and came in a day early to do Media. I didn't work with Willie, as he was **CBS** baggage and he didn't do any backstage stuff either, just stayed in his bus doing what keeps Willie up til it was time to hit the stage.

Waylon was very amiable to work with, and the big thing we did was a photo shoot for one of the daily papers at the front of the Vancouver Art Gallery for the next day's front page. Yes! Waylon was impressed.

The next morning, neither of us was impressed to **NOT** see his photo on the front page; we were upstaged by a Clown, a goddam CLOWN! So, what do you say to the artist when THAT happens?!...um, well, he was funnier than you, Mr. Lonesome, Onery and Mean! AND, you have 25 people riding in 3 Buses and trucks, the Clown has that many in ONE CAR!...or something.

What else I didn't know that day prior to winding up with Seltzer on my face first thing in the morning was that **Waylon & Willie** had snuck away for a round of golf, first stop, the **Point Grey Golf Club**! A VERY high-end (that may have attracted Willie) place that took one look at these two Raggedy–ass Red Necks and summarily ran them off the property; the nerve! The Point Grey people had NO idea who these two were. So, next stop, **Musqueum Golf Course,** a lot more Salt-of-the-Earth (or rim) atmosphere, and after a great round of golf they went to the clubhouse and were buying rounds and the tipping staff $50s and $100s, and Willie invited everyone down to **Pedernales**, his Golf Course in Texas, to play for FREE, anytime!

The newspapers got onto this at the speed of light and the Point Grey Snooty-toot-toot Golf Course got more unwanted publicity than they could handle, Rich People being in the Minority. Now, what was that about a book and its cover?

Yeah.

Here's Raylon and Waylon backstage at The Coliseum in 1984 in conversation: Where's Willie? On the Bus. What's he doin'? High-ding.
Photo by Bev Davies

KITTY WELLS-

Ironically, I met her in a Honky-Tonk, the Rootin' Tootin' Newton Inn, and she *was* an Angel, just not the one in the song she made famous.

WHITE RABBIT-

Classic, Vintage **Jefferson Airplane**, a great track.

Their original singer, **Signe Anderson,** missed the boat, or at least the Airplane; she was singed, but not charred, by the coming success.

Her replacement was **Grace Slick,** who brought this track to **Jefferson Airplane,** written by her (then) husband Darby, who wrote it for *his* band,

The Great Society. So, while he wasn't singed, he wasn't burned either, as this little mind-blower made a fair chunk of change for him.

It's rare to hear a song with this arrangement/structure, a straight build, right to the climatic end; no verse/chorus, just straight from the floor up (up and away!) with a soaring starburst climax.

THAT kind of writing is actually a throwback to **Roy Orbison**. He was a Genius with his styles, and "**Running Scared**" is an excellent example of the Big Build, big finish.

But we didn't know that back then; those songs weren't so unique as "new." Pop music was still developing, but *NOW*, by comparison to all that went before, the trite/true combo of Verse/chorus/bridge/repeat and out, **that** song and those like it are truly unique.

Roy was an original **Original**, and later, "**White Rabbit**" stands in the same light, especially given the Alice-in-Mind-Blasted-Land subject matter.

The Fabs made good use of BOTH techniques with a verse/chorus, verse/chorus Big Build with a spine-tingling chant/mantra, primal scream with Heavenly choir finish for the unforgettable "**Hey Jude**"; it was almost exhausting. Not to forget the dark crescendo ending of "**A day in the life**" and too many more.

All great, brilliant, masterpieces; good for chasing rabbits…

THE WHO-

Never met them BUT I was involved with one of their concerts here when **Bruce Allen's** master stroke of getting **Powder Blues** on the show as the opener happened. This prompted me to issue a Press Release to God and EVERYONE that **The Who** would be *closing* the show for *them*. THAT bit of cheek got us some attention, uh huh.

WILBUR HARRISON-

You might call this segment "Playing shorthanded."

Wilbur hit it big in 1959 when his "**Kansas City**" went to #1 on the Pop Charts (later to be covered by **The Beatles**), and a few years later he hit the charts again with "**Let's work together**."

I got to see Wilbur in concert opening for **Lee Michaels** at The Pacific Coliseum. This is where the "shorthanded" part comes in…He was a One-Man Band!

Lee Michaels, the Headliner, was playing with only a drummer, '**Frosty**' (Bartholomew Smith-Frost) and they were superlative, Lee & awesome Frosty!

So between the TWO acts in a near full arena, there were THREE people on stage performing, and not all at once.

After a few minor albums, Lee hit his stride with his "*5th*" then "*Live*" albums which produced "**Heighty Hi**," "**Do You Know What I Mean?** and "**Can I Get a Witness**".

I didn't get to meet Lee, altho TPC distributed his label, A&M, they had their own Reps, but I sure dug that concert, those albums, and Frosty's drumming; you can't beat it.

ROGER WHITTAKER-

The **Zulu** uprising survivor and Grand Old Gentleman of Easy Listening and Postum addict. What a treat to work with.

Here we all are in 1984 on the set of the **Don Harron Show/BCTV** *giving Roger "Wind Beneath My Wings" Whittaker a Multiple Platinum Sales Award. L>R: Roger, Don Harron, R's truly with the wind at my back, and the late Leagh "Wind Beneath My Pants" Alden (RCA) trying to not drop the award on his foot.*

CHATTER #36

HANK WILLIAMS-

Died before I was 6, but I DID meet with his backing band **The Drifting Cowboys,** who were then backing his son **Hank Jr. (Bocephus)** pre-fall from mountain, and **Sheb Wooley (Ben Colder)** 50s star for "**Purple People Eater.**" They were both a good experience, especially later when Hank stepped out of his Dad's boots and into his own. At that show, he insisted that I go on his bus and have a look around. Good guy, Great talent.

From Son to the Father, hmmm, wonder who THIS is about...

Reco-"Blues Man" and almost everything else

MICHELLE WRIGHT-

Cat Suit Woman. Among the nicest you could meet; Genuine. The **FIRST** signing to **Arista Nashville,** the last to get a hit. Putting some bite into "**You Owe Me**" would have had Shania looking over her shoulder. Her cats, Marge & Homer, never had a better Mom.

I worked with her since 1977 to 2004 and am pleased to say she's one of Canada's own.

Reco- Michelle Wright. "Shut Up and Kiss Me," "He Would Be 16," "Strong"

A message from Michelle to my wife...

Michelle and R's truly

YES-

Possibly best known for wearing loose clothing with poofy sleeves and Capes and stuff while riding a "**Roundabout**." Less well known was **Jon Anderson's** backstage dressing room, which was a Tepee (that's right Kien Sabe!). Band and crew would sneak up and pin stuffed animals and plush toys to it, which upset the head Yes Man.

Even lesser known was the band's penchant for massive intakes of outrageously priced wine at other people's expense. It became something of a contest to them in fact. I heard about this behavior and decided to act.

Knowing nothing about wine, my favorite being **Budweiser**, aside from price, I couldn't tell a good one from a bad one, but a BAD one was what I was looking for and found it! I wrapped it all up nicely, and the band seemed impressed that I would think of them and put it aside to be opened post-concert. I wasn't there for that, of course, but it would be priceless to see their faces after opening a bottle of "**Old Porch Climber**" served with six straws. **BINGO!**

YANNI-

The "**Aria**" track went OVER THE TOP. Who would have believed an A3, MOR (Middle of the Road) artist would top the **#1 Top 40 station here (Z95)?! Matthew McBride** did that. It went GOLD, Jerry, GOLD!

Reco- Yanni, – "Aria"

WARREN ZEVON-

Truly a tortured soul and something of a creative Musical Genius.

The **Wolf Man** had his big hit, and it was really well written and remains an enduring Classic and not just in October. He was a very strong if underappreciated writer.

One of his best efforts is **"Poor Poor Pitiful Me,"** which he wrote and recorded in 1976. **Linda Ronstadt's** version, which came later, may be the best version that I've heard; the chorus and the guitar run at the end are superb, and it segues well with the **Rolling Stones' "Brown Sugar"** (another guitar masterpiece; how many tracks Keith?), which is one of the BEST Rock songs ever written, in my estimation, and seeing as it's me that's writing this, the Defense rests.

I didn't get to meet Warren in person; I met him on the phone one day when I was calling **"Odd's" Craig Northey**. and he passed the call to Warren and we chatted, which was more like him exhorting me to meet him downtown and we'd get drunk and some *whores!* So, high and low I guess, but I took a Rain Cheque.

Craig explained that **Odds** were to be Warren's band at his **"86 Street"** concert. and the Odds found out what Warren would be wearing that night and went out and bought the exact same thing, so when Warren walked onstage, he saw everybody dressed in Black T-Shirts and Powder Blue Jeans. He took one look at them and asked if they were **Lou Reed's** band! Walk on the Mild side.

Linda Ronstadt did a Primo job of one of Warren's finest. I noticed a difference in lyrics between Warren's version and Linda's, and my friend **Craig Northey** (of '**Odds**') , having worked with Warren, explained while he had a fabulous sense of humor, some of it was too dark and went unappreciated, so Linda made an executrix decision and lightened it up with her own bright sense of humor

A tortured soul and a torte soul…

Reco- Linda Ronstadt, "Poor Poor Pitiful Me"

Reco- Warren Zevon, "Werewolves of London"

LISA ZBITNEW-

Wow.

*(L>R) Do I really have to do that? There's only two people; **REALLY?**
OK, Lisa Z and Me at my "Let's Throw Raymond from the Gravy Train" fete.
Shooter-Dee Lippingwell*

BMG Canada's "First Lady" and a BIG supporter of yours truly. Awarded me the prestigious **"President's Award,"** the company's highest honor (No, I WON'T stop bigging this up!). That, and her letter to me, also framed, hang in the Ramseum next to the **"Inspiration"** and other myriad awards.

That's who I was; ask any young person today about me, and they'll tell you in NO uncertain terms...he's the old gray guy, right? (Sniff!), Yes, thank you, very observant.

These are only a few of the ones I **Raymember** and they are **ALL Special** to me in a way that transcends definition.

Ray Ramsay

CPSIA information can be obtained
at www.ICGtesting.com
Printed in the USA
BVHW021845230622
640466BV00004B/10